Augustus

So mighty was the name of Augustus, first Roman emperor and adopted son and heir of Julius Caesar, that the Roman month of Sextilis was renamed in his honour. Matthew Clark's accessible volume brings to life the political manoeuvring of this key figure in Roman history and helps us understand his relationships with the most eminent politicians, generals and poets of the day. He emerges as the classical world's true master of 'spin', demonstrating that political propaganda is far from just a modern phenomenon.

Matthew Clark teaches classics at Shrewsbury School. He is co-author of *Measuring the Cosmos* (2003) and reviews regularly for *Journal of Classics Teaching*.

The Prima Porta statue of Augustus

AUGUSTUS
FIRST ROMAN EMPEROR

POWER, PROPAGANDA AND
THE POLITICS OF SURVIVAL

Matthew D.H. Clark

BRISTOL
PHOENIX
PRESS

Cover image: 'Audience with Agrippa' by Sir Lawrence Alma-Tadema
(reproduced courtesy of East Ayrshire Council Museums,
Arts and Theatre Service)

First published in 2010 by
Bristol Phoenix Press
an imprint of The Exeter Press
Reed Hall, Streatham Drive
Exeter EX4 4QR
UK
www.exeterpress.co.uk

British Library Cataloguing in Publication Data
A catalogue record for this book is available from the British Library.

Hardback ISBN 978 1 904675 43 3
Paperback ISBN 978 1 904675 14 3

Typeset in Chaparral Pro 11.5pt on 15pt
by JCS Publishing Services Ltd

Printed in Great Britain by Short Run Press Ltd

Contents

ILLUSTRATIONS

Illustrations

Maps

Many thanks to my colleague, Toby Percival, for providing the photos to illustrate this book.

Author's Note on Roman Names

When there is a well-known English version of a Roman name, I have used this in my narrative to help the general reader. Thus I have used Pompey for Gnaeus Pompeius Magnus (Pompey the Great), Mark Antony for Marcus Antonius and Virgil for Vergilius etc.

The Roman Empire in the time of Augustus

CASPIAN SEA

E

E

G

BLACK SEA

Tomis

Danube

ARMENIA

O E S I A

BITHYNIA-PONTUS

Amaseia

Byzantium

Ancyra

MESOPOTAMIA

EDONIA

GALATIA

Phillipi

P A R T H I A

Thessalonica

CILICIA

Euphrates

lus

m

Tarsus

Antioch

A S I A

SYRIA

A C H A I A

Ephesus

Athen

RHODES

CYPRUS

Tyre

IUDAEA

CRETA

Jerusalem

ARABIA

NTERNUM MARE

Alexandria

Pelusium

Cyrene

Memphis

CYRENAICA

E

G

Y

P

RED SEA

T

Nile

E   R   T

Italy in the time of Augustus

INTRODUCTION

'BOY, YOU OWE EVERYTHING TO YOUR NAME'

M odern political observers are fascinated by the relationship between power and presentation. Communication
directors and 'spin doctors' can now become as famous as the
politicians they work for. We often assume that propaganda and
political presentation are a modern art, dependent on the mass
media, such as film and television. Yet we can observe many of
the same political strategies in both the literary and the archaeo-
logical sources for Augustan Rome that we see in the modern
world of politics. In fact, it was not a commanding military figure
– such as Pompey or Julius Caesar – who had the most lasting
historical legacy in the first century BC, but rather Augustus, the
master of politics and propaganda.

In his *Annals* (I.9f), the great Roman historian Tacitus provides
a summary of Augustus' career, which makes an excellent
starting point for considering both his unique achievements
and his particular ruthlessness. Tacitus contrasts the views
of the admirers of Augustus with those of his critics. Most
historians believe that Tacitus fundamentally agreed with the
latter party; he wrote with the benefit of hindsight and he had
experienced how the Augustan principate had degenerated into
autocracy under his successors. Tacitus' personal perspective was
influenced by the early years of his career under the tyrannical
Emperor Domitian.

In the first half of his discussion, Tacitus points out that Augustus had held the consulship more times than any other Roman, and that he had held 'tribunician power' (eventually Augustus' most significant title) continuously for 37 years. His admirers excused the excesses of his early years on account of the desperate circumstances of the Civil War and his filial duty to avenge his father. Julius Caesar had adopted Augustus as his son in his will, but the distinction between a natural and adopted son was not an important one for the Romans. Furthermore, as readers of Virgil's *Aeneid* will know, '*pietas*' (best translated in this context as family loyalty) was the highest Roman virtue.

The apologists for Augustus excused his autocracy by claiming that the only possible cure for the diseases faced by the Roman Empire was rule by one man. Yet Augustus had implemented this autocracy, not with provocative traditional titles such as king (*rex*) or dictator, but by the inoffensive title, *princeps*, meaning first citizen. Tacitus understood that the conciliatory language surrounding Augustus' power was significant.

Augustus' defenders robustly point to the healthy state of the empire on Augustus' death. The frontiers of the empire had been extended and secured, and were now based on the geographical boundaries of oceans or mighty rivers. The majesty of Roman law protected its citizens. This was no mean achievement. As we can see from the travels of St Paul in the New Testament in the first century AD, a Roman citizen could safely travel the length of the empire, secure in the protection of his citizenship. Rome itself was transformed with magnificent decoration. These Augustan loyalists admit that a few problems had been dealt with by force, but only to secure a peaceful life for the majority.

However, Tacitus followed this summary of Augustan spin with a cynical analysis of Augustus' real motives and biting criticism of his career (*Annals*, I.10). As Tacitus was writing around 100 years after Augustus' death, he was in no personal danger in doing this, but this analysis was still potentially subversive of the imperial system of the emperors of his own day, such as Trajan and Hadrian. The critics of Augustus whispered that his real motivation had always been lust for power. He had used bribery and hypocrisy to reach the summit of authority. He had used illegal violence, and perhaps even hidden assassination to achieve his ends. He had shown treachery to his former allies, and had even exploited his sister to reach supreme power. These unnamed critics acknowledged that after his victories Augustus had presided over a period of peace, but they described it ironically as a 'blood-stained peace' (*cruentam pacem*) (*Annals*, I.10). This peace was stained with costly defeats on the German frontier and by the ruthless elimination of political opponents.

This critical analysis moves on to accuse Augustus of hypocrisy. On the one hand he advocated a return to traditional Roman morality, but on the other his own personal life was controversial, especially his marriage to Livia, who had been married previously to another senator. Augustus also had some disreputable friends, such as Publius Vedius Pollio, whom we know from other sources made a habit of feeding his slaves to his eels. (Even by Roman standards of cruelty this was regarded as excessive, but that was simply a matter of personal distaste, rather than a crime.) The final damaging criticism is that Augustus chose Livia's son Tiberius as his heir, not because he believed that Tiberius was the best available man for the job, but so that Augustus' own glory would be highlighted by the inferior quality of his successor.

Tacitus' summary shows us that we are dealing with a historical figure who can be judged in completely different ways. No other Roman had such a long-lasting historical legacy; not Julius Caesar, Rome's great soldier, not Cicero, Rome's greatest orator. Augustus' political career lasted for 58 years, and throughout that time he survived within a dangerous and competitive political culture.

The Augustan principate produced strong central government for over 200 years from 30 BC until AD 180. The political structures he put in place could survive mad emperors and civil wars. Even after the great days of the Roman Empire, Augustus' rule represented a model to aspire to; senators prayed that their emperors could be 'more fortunate than Augustus and better than Trajan' (prayer of the Roman Senate in the third century AD). Their wish was seldom granted.

Yet these achievements in government came at a price. There were previous Roman leaders who were as ruthless as Augustus, but none was so professional in the art of politics. If Machiavelli had searched for a model for a successful competitor in the joust of politics, he could have chosen no better figure than Augustus. Augustus was in no way an outstanding military leader. One of his wisest choices was to recognise that the closest friend of his youth, Marcus Vipsanius Agrippa, was far more able in this field. Nevertheless, he had a shrewd understanding of the different classes of the Roman Republic, and took great care to build as big a tent of supporters as possible. However, he made sure that any opposition was crushed. In his rise to power he was brutal in disposing of his enemies, and he became particularly skilled in picking them off one by one. His favoured technique, which he used many times, was to make his enemies' armies mutiny in his favour. He achieved this by use of skilled subversive agents and by outbidding his opponents in the auction for the loyalties of their soldiers. Once he had achieved the summit of power he became more surgical, but he nevertheless built up a highly effective intelligence service. He was more than happy to launch a pre-emptive political strike on anyone who even raised the possibility of opposition to his power.

One important fact that strikes anyone studying the history of the late Roman Republic from 79 BC until 30 BC is that it was incredibly dangerous to pursue a career in the forefront of Rome's politics. Any list of the most prominent Roman senators of this period would include Pompey, Crassus, Julius Caesar, Cicero, Catiline, Clodius, Milo, Domitius Ahenobarbus, Cato, Mark Antony, Marcus Brutus and Gaius Cassius. These 12 men covered the political spectrum from reactionary conservatives through conciliatory trimmers to ardent populists. Some were great orators, others were great soldiers. Their names fill the letters of Cicero, the reports of Julius Caesar and the plays of Shakespeare. The one thing they all have in common is that they died violently. The exception is Marcus Licinius Crassus who died fighting a foreign enemy; all the rest died either through political violence or fighting in civil war. Death squads and private armies had become an accepted risk for ambition. Sulla in 80 BC was the last leader of the Roman Republic to die in his bed. Augustus learnt this lesson well. Even Tacitus' critique cannot mask the point that Augustus died old, and that by AD 14 membership of Rome's senate had become rather less perilous.

An interesting demonstration of Augustus' careful use of political vocabulary was the attention that he paid to his personal name. He changed his name on several occasions to fit the political climate. This makes life rather awkward for students and scholars of the late republic, and the usual convention, which I will also follow, is to refer to our hero as Augustus when considering the whole of his life, but as Octavian when referring to events before 27 BC. The reality, as discussed by Suetonius (*Twelve Caesars*, Augustus, 7), was rather more complex. In his infancy he was known as Gaius Octavius Thurinus, taking the first two names from his father, who was a popular senator originating from an equestrian family and who rose up the *cursus honorum* (the honours race) as far as the praetorship before his untimely death. The name Thurinus perhaps came from his father's successes against runaway slaves near Thurii. Suetonius elegantly establishes this as Augustus' infant *cognomen* by his discovery of a bronze statuette, which he says that he himself presented to the Emperor Hadrian. Mark Antony used this name as a form of abuse during the war of words before the Actium campaign, to which Octavian ingenuously replied that he was surprised that his childhood name should be thought at all discreditable.

The young Gaius Octavius moved dramatically into the public world of Roman politics when he was adopted as Julius Caesar's heir. As was usual in such cases, Gaius Octavius took on the name Gaius Julius Caesar, following the instructions of his great-uncle's will. This is the point where modern historians usually call him Octavian, and he did on occasion call himself Gaius Julius Caesar Octavianus, but this simplification sacrifices an important aspect of the political reality. The name 'Gaius Julius Caesar' was vital to recruit troops, money and followers in the desperate days following Julius Caesar's assassination. When Julius Caesar was acknowledged as a god, after a dramatic comet appeared over Rome in 43 BC, Octavian took on the new title '*divi filius*', son of the deified Caesar. This claim to be the son of a god certainly gave his camp glamour and helped him to attract more followers and more money than the other claimants to the leadership of the Caesarian party such as Lepidus or Mark Antony. It was as Gaius Julius Caesar, son of the deified Julius, that he led the forces that won the battle of Actium under the military instructions of his most valuable colleague, Marcus Agrippa.

The changed circumstances of sole rule that followed this victory led in turn to Octavian taking a new name. With his inner circle, men such as Agrippa and Gaius Cilnius Maecenas, he debated whether he should assume the name of Romulus as a second founder of the city. This name would have carried negative overtones of the monarchy that had been discredited in Rome's early history and would certainly have repeated the offence caused to upper-class Romans by Julius Caesar's confrontational title of 'dictator perpetuus'. Instead, Lucius Munatius Plancus suggested that he assume the name Augustus. Plancus is one of the very few senior Roman figures of the republic to survive into the new era. He managed this by a number of astute changes of side at vital moments, and gained the reputation of being a good luck charm. Thus it was significant that he had deserted Antony for Octavian shortly before the Actium campaign. In the Senate, Plancus argued with typical agility that the title of Augustus was both honourable and original. He quoted Rome's most venerated poet Ennius to demonstrate the resonance of this new name (Suetonius, *The Twelve Caesars*, Augustus, 7).

Thus Mark Antony's observation that Augustus owed everything to his name, quoted in the title to this introduction (Cicero, *Philippics*, 13.11.24–5) was not merely applicable to his rise to power in 43 BC, but remained true throughout his career. Augustus' careful projection of his image through his name, as Suetonius explains at the beginning of his biography of Augustus (Suetonius, *Twelve Caesars*, Augustus, 7), was deliberate and considered policy. As I discuss Augustus' career in more detail I hope to demonstrate the depth of his policies of propaganda and to show that his use of his name was merely one feature of his sophisticated political strategy. Augustus' mastery of the dark arts of manipulating public opinion and controlling the verdict of history was vital for his own survival and his success in establishing a stable form of government for the Roman Empire.

PART I

THE FAILURE OF THE
ROMAN REPUBLIC

CHAPTER 1

THE STRAINS OF EMPIRE

In order to put Augustus' career and achievements into perspective we need to have a good understanding of the preceding history of the Roman Republic. By the time of Augustus' birth this republic had gained control of a vast Mediterranean empire. However, it was precisely Rome's success that caused the Roman state to come apart in a series of civil wars. Thus a brief narrative of the failure of the Roman Republic helps to illustrate the extent of Augustus' Roman revolution.

Roman legend recounted that Romulus founded the city of Rome in 753 BC, and shortly afterwards killed his twin brother Remus. Romulus was recorded as the first of seven kings of which the last was Tarquinius the Proud. Roman tradition then said that Tarquinius was deposed by a popular revolt because of his own despotic behaviour and because of the unpopularity of his sons. The early legends are not at all reliable, and even our sources for the end of the monarchy are much later than the events they describe, but it is usually believed that the Roman Republic dates back to around 510 BC. Thus by the time of the birth of Augustus in 63 BC, the republican institutions had evolved over hundreds of years. The Roman upper class created an effective oligarchy preserving the dominant influence of a small number of families. This political system was celebrated by historians such as Polybius, and regarded as venerable and sacred by politicians such as Cato and Cicero. The challenge that Augustus faced was to maintain the façade of the republican system while replacing a competitive oligarchy with stable authoritarian rule.

The Roman Republic is historically important because of its dramatic military success. In 500 BC Rome was simply one of a number of flourishing cities in Italy. Roman power extended gradually. It took over 200 years for Rome to gain control over southern Italy. The expansion of Roman government beyond Italy and across the Mediterranean was primarily a result of the wars against her bitterest rival, the city of Carthage in north Africa, which had also acquired an empire in the Western Mediterranean. The Romans and the Carthaginians initially clashed in 264 BC over the control of Sicily. The conflicts between the two city-states escalated in intensity, leading to the invasion of Italy by Hannibal after an epic journey with his forces across the Alps. Hannibal won a series of devastating victories against the Romans, most famously at the battle of Cannae. Yet he lacked the manpower and siege equipment to capture the city of Rome itself despite maintaining an army in Italy for 15 years. Eventually the Romans produced a commander, Scipio Africanus, who could match Hannibal's tactical mastery. Scipio won a series of battles in Spain and then invaded Africa. He eventually forced Hannibal to retreat from Italy; Scipio at last managed to beat Hannibal and his exhausted veterans at the battle of Zama in north Africa, and the war was ended on terms that established the supremacy of Rome in the western Mediterranean.

The victory over Hannibal represented the greatest achievement of the Roman Republic. Despite terrible defeats the Romans maintained the support of their Italian allies and continued to raise large armies. The Roman Senate provided strong leadership for the state and was eventually able to choose commanders with sufficient ability to prevail against a formidable enemy. The victories against the Carthaginians caused the Romans to set up provinces in Sicily and Sardinia, and also in Spain. However, once Rome was free from the competition of her most dangerous rival, her system of government came under strain.

The next phase of Roman expansion took place in the Eastern Mediterranean. The Romans were drawn into a series of wars against Hellenistic monarchs who wanted to challenge the power of the expanding republic. The Roman legions won a series of decisive victories against the Macedonian phalanx formation, and between 149 BC and 146 BC Rome created the provinces of Macedonia and Achaea. Also in 146 BC the Romans finally destroyed Carthage, after creating a pretext for conflict, and formed a new province in Africa (initially covering the area of modern Tunisia). In 133 BC Roman territory expanded further, when King Attalus III of Pergamum left his kingdom to Rome in his will. This was a shrewd method of avoiding Roman annexation and civil war, and this territory became the new Roman province of Asia in modern western Turkey.

These military and diplomatic victories created an extensive empire and changed Roman society forever. Rome became much wealthier, but the increase in wealth was shared neither equally nor equitably. Historians such as Sallust (*War with Catiline*, 10) traced the decline in the standard of civic virtue in the upper classes from the end of the Roman rivalry with Carthage and from the contact with the Greek East. The victorious commanders and their families became hugely wealthy and the Roman senators set new standards of luxury inspired by the example of the Hellenistic monarchs. Augustus would try to set limits on the level of decadence in Roman society but without success.

Another vital economic change was the vast influx of slaves into Italy as captives from the various wars of conquest. This meant that wealthy landowners could earn huge profits from their large estates. On the other hand, many Italian peasant farmers spent years serving in Rome's legions overseas. For many smallholders the only economic option was to sell their land to a wealthy landowner and to move to Rome. This process created a vicious circle of the rich getting richer and the poor getting poorer. This economic instability lay behind the hundred years of political turmoil between 133 BC and the final victory of Augustus in 30 BC.

There were also important political factors that made the late republic so unstable. By 133 BC Rome's republican constitution had evolved over more than 300 years to reflect the interests of the different classes in Rome. The Romans were very concerned to build checks and balances into their system and they wanted to prevent the tyranny of kings such as Tarquinius Superbus. The very word *rex* became abhorrent to them.

The Greek historian Polybius (*Histories*, VI.11.11), writing in the third century BC, described Rome's constitution as incorporating the best of monarchy, oligarchy and democracy. The element of monarchy was reflected in the power of the two consuls, who were the supreme magistrates in Rome for their year in office. The risk of a single tyrant was avoided and the short period of office was designed to prevent any individuals from gaining excessive power. This Roman hatred of autocracy was the essential factor that led to the assassination of Julius Caesar, and Augustus made great efforts to make his authority palatable to all the different classes in both Rome and Italy. The consulship was merely the pinnacle of a complicated system of official offices known by the Romans as the *cursus honorum*. The competition to reach the higher levels of office was intense, and the most important election each year was the one that determined the two consuls.

The element of democracy in the Roman constitution was fulfilled by the assemblies and by the tribunes. There were two particularly important assemblies of citizens: the Comitia Centuriata (Assembly of Centuries) and the Comitia Tributa (Tribal Assembly). The Comitia Centuriata's main function was to elect Rome's senior magistrates each year. The people voted in a complex system of military centuries that favoured the wealthier classes. In order to be elected consul or praetor, the annual civic magistrates in Rome, it was especially important to have a solid base of support in the class known as the *equites* (the equestrian class, or knights)—men who owned property worth more than 400,000 sesterces. The *equites* were the wealthy Roman citizens who had not held office as senators, and they made up the upper-middle class. Their support was crucial for any ambitious politician. On occasion they could be roused to oppose the corruption of the Senate; at other times, they acted in support of the Senate to maintain their own privileges. Augustus established a good relationship with the *equites* and developed particular posts for them to serve the empire.

The importance of the Tribal Assembly was that it had the power to pass laws binding on the Roman state. The 'tribes' that voted in this assembly were groups of the Roman population, based on residence and traditional family ties. The distribution of the Roman citizens in these tribes was rather unequal and gave the rural population a disproportionate influence. However, there was some scope in the Tribal Assembly for more radical politicians to exploit popular discontent. The agrarian laws, passed in this assembly, were used in the late republic to grant land to poorer citizens and veteran soldiers, and to give extraordinary military commands to famous generals. Politicians known as *populares*, who wanted to gain favour with the poorer classes in Rome, would use this assembly to ratify their policies. Thus there was great potential for conflict between politicians known as the *optimates*, who sought to safeguard the supremacy of the Senate, and these *populares*.

This competition was intensified by the role of the tribunes. In the early years of the republic, the patricians (a small group of aristocratic families) dominated political power. The rest of the Roman population, known as the plebeians, campaigned for their own representatives and succeeded in establishing the post of the tribunes. Each year ten tribunes were elected to represent the plebeians. Patricians were prevented from standing for this post. The tribunes gradually obtained more powers as the republic developed. Any one tribune could veto any action by the state that he considered to be against the interest of the people. The tribunes could propose laws in the Tribal Assembly that were passed if they received the backing of a majority of the tribes. They were immune from prosecution while they held office. Augustus took advantage of this tradition of the tribunes acting as the guardians of the people by creating for himself *tribunicia potestas* (tribunician power) that allowed him to propose laws before the Senate and the assemblies and which gave him a position as the protector of the citizens of Rome. The *tribunicia potestas* became one of his most important sources of authority.

Given that each tribune had the power of veto, it might be considered surprising that the Roman state ever acted decisively. However, the tribunes were usually young men who were ambitious to develop a career in the Senate themselves. As the republic grew wealthier and more powerful, so some plebeian families attained the status of nobility. Thus they became just as anxious as the patricians to maintain the authority of the Senate. Most tribunes were concerned not to rock the boat and thus the use of veto was rare before the dramatic careers of the brothers Tiberius and Gaius Gracchus at the end of the second century BC.

The element of oligarchy was reflected in the power of the Roman Senate. Candidates who gained office as magistrates in the republic received a place in the Senate. They surrendered their office at the end of that year, but they retained the rank from their position throughout their lives, and with it their place in the Senate. The Senate gradually gained more and more authority as the only permanent political institution in Rome. The most influential members of the Senate were the ex-consuls, who maintained their influence not by virtue of any particular office, but because of their *auctoritas* (authority). Augustus preserved the prestige of the Senate but he reduced its level of independent power. Instead, his own personal *auctoritas* was such that he took all the crucial decisions for the Roman state.

Under the republic, provincial governors were appointed from the members of the Senate, usually immediately after they had finished their year in office as consuls or praetors. Within their own provinces, governors had the ultimate authority. Corruption was widespread, since many senators had fallen heavily into debt in order to get elected as magistrates in the first place. Oppressed provincials could seldom even rely on the protection of Roman law. Before 123 BC (and also from 82 BC to 70 BC), provincial governors were tried before a court of their fellow senators, who had a strong interest in acquitting their colleagues in case they themselves might come up before such a court.

The most renowned example of a corrupt governor was Gaius Verres, who was in authority over Sicily for three years (73–71 BC). Verres was supposed to have claimed that in his first year he would extort enough money to pay for his election bribes, his second year would cover the money he would need to bribe his future jury, and in the third year he would make some profit for himself. Verres was so careless in his embezzlement that he harmed some friends of Pompey the Great (Gnaeus Pompeius

Magnus), the most powerful Roman of the day. Thus Cicero had plenty of support when he prosecuted Verres, which meant he was able to secure a guilty verdict. Such a conviction was unusual, and only followed the most flagrant abuses of power. As a result, the system of governing the provinces was held in disrepute throughout the late republic. Augustus made great efforts to improve the honesty of provincial government. Any provincial governor who exceeded his authority became accountable to him.

However, the threat to the structure of the Roman Republic came not from corrupt governors, nor from provincial revolt, but from the power of individual generals in the provinces. Rome's imperial wars led to the need for huge armies in the provinces. Yet there was little central control of their pay or of their discharge. The tradition grew up that the victorious general would organise a grant of land for retiring troops. The legionaries developed a much stronger loyalty to their individual commanders than to the central state. Furthermore, Roman law ensured that the state would hold no armies in Italy itself. Thus when provincial commanders threatened to lead an army into Italy, the Senate was defenceless. Augustus' great achievement was to establish a political system that could administer Rome's vast empire peacefully.

CHAPTER 2

THE DEATH OF THE REPUBLIC

A ll the economic and political weaknesses of the republic were exposed in a hundred years of civil conflict before Augustus' final political settlement. The young aristocrat Tiberius Gracchus was elected tribune in 133 BC on the manifesto of reallocating state-owned land to the poorer classes. This proposal was moderate in itself and Gracchus intended to ensure that the Roman armies could maintain their level of manpower. He ran into bitter resistance since wealthy senators occupied much of this land illegally. Tiberius Gracchus responded energetically against this opposition. He aimed to overthrow the veto of a fellow tribune and tried to be re-elected for a further year. Eventually a conservative senator called Scipio Nasica organised a lynch mob that killed Tiberius Gracchus and 300 of his supporters. This was the most violent civil strife in Rome since the founding of the republic.

Ten years later, Tiberius' younger brother, Gaius Gracchus, tried to revive the programme of reform. Not surprisingly, Gaius Gracchus was better prepared and more confrontational towards the Senate. He served as tribune for two years and carried out a number of radical measures such as reintroducing his brother's proposal for land redistribution and transferring the courts from the control of the senators to the *equites*. He also raised the issue of whether Rome's Latin allies should receive the full Roman citizenship. In 121 BC the consul Opimius led a military force against Gaius Gracchus and his supporters. Gaius Gracchus suffered the same fate as his brother, and thousands of his supporters were executed without trial.

The next crisis for the Roman republic resulted from the clashes of the political factions led by Marius and Sulla. Gaius Marius, despite being a *novus homo* (new man) without senatorial ancestors, was Rome's leading military commander from 107 BC until 100 BC. He reacted to difficulties in Africa and the German frontier by abandoning Rome's traditional policy of recruiting soldiers from the landowning classes. Instead, he enlisted volunteers from both the urban and rural poor. This solved the initial problem diagnosed by Tiberius Gracchus but it accentuated the drift towards further unconstitutional power for the commanders of the legions. These landless troops were prepared to follow their commanders even if they defied the will of the Roman Senate and people.

A conflict later known as the Social War broke out between Rome and some of its Italian allies in 91 BC over the issue of access to full Roman citizenship. After some initial defeats the Romans successfully kept control over Italy by granting concessions to loyal communities and by crushing their armed opponents in battle. Both Sulla and Marius commanded Roman armies in this period but they came to represent opposed political groups within Rome. Marius had been elected consul in 107 BC. Although he was more moderate than Gaius Gracchus, he was sympathetic to some policies of reform, particularly in the military sphere. The senatorial class had been forced to tolerate him because he seemed the only general who could deliver military victories against the foreign enemies that threatened the republic's frontiers. However, a younger general named Sulla became increasingly identified with the cause of the supremacy of the Senate. He aimed to prevent any constitutional change and to

pursue his own political interests. Once he had demonstrated in the Social War that he was a match for Marius on the battlefield, he became a focus of support for senators determined to prevent any erosion of their privileged position.

The rivalry between the Sullans and the Marians came to a head in 88 BC. The two factions clashed over whether Sulla or Marius should lead the army against Mithridates, King of Pontus, who had invaded the eastern provinces. Sulla was the obvious choice as he had been elected consul and he could take over the army at the end of his year in office. Furthermore, he was a much younger man. Marius had been a great commander 12 years before, but he was now elderly. However, a popular movement led by the tribune Sulpicius advocated that Marius should take over this lucrative command. In return Marius promised to support Sulpicius to pass a programme of radical legislation in the spirit of Gaius Gracchus. Marius and Sulpicius used the urban mob to support their cause and Sulla withdrew from the city.

Sulla was not prepared, though, to accept defeat quietly. He moved swiftly to take over the army, which was assembling south of Rome at Nola in Campania. He took the radical step— then unprecedented in Rome's history—of leading six legions, (approximately 30,000 men) into the city of Rome. This broke a sacred tradition that no Roman should lead an army into the city boundaries. It is ironic that a reactionary conservative such as Sulla broke this tradition, but he no doubt felt justified by the danger that the alliance of Sulpicius and Marius posed to the senatorial order. Sulpicius was hunted down and killed despite his privileged position as a tribune. The elderly Marius escaped to the province of Africa. Sulla declared all of Sulpicius' laws invalid and led his forces to fight Mithridates on the eastern frontier as he had initially planned.

Marius was not finished yet; in Sulla's absence he conspired with Cinna, one of the consuls, to take over Rome. He launched a reign of terror against Sulla's supporters and ruined his reputation as a moderate by carrying out a large number of arbitrary executions. Marius died a few days after beginning his seventh consulship and Cinna and his supporter Carbo—another *popularis* politician—took control of the Marian faction.

Meanwhile Sulla was successful in his campaign against Mithridates. In 85 BC he signed a favourable treaty and prepared his army to retake Italy. Cinna tried to organise military resistance but was killed by some of his own soldiers who were rioting because of lack of pay. Sulla landed in southern Italy in 83 BC. Carbo and Marius' son became consuls for the next year and they tried to rally the popular forces against Sulla, but he gained the support of most of the senators and many others, who realised that he was the likely victor of this struggle. Younger men such as Crassus and Pompey, who would be important figures in the next phase of the republic's history, joined Sulla's forces. He was victorious in the decisive battle at the Colline Gate outside Rome and massacred many of his prisoners within earshot of the Roman Senate.

Sulla cemented his control over Italy by launching the proscriptions. He used the Latin word *proscriptiones* as a euphemism for the death lists in which he ordered the murder of numerous political opponents. He confiscated their property to reward his soldiers and supporters. One ancient historian, Orosius, estimated that Sulla ordered the deaths of 9,000 wealthy citizens (Scullard, *From the Gracchi to Nero*, p. 79). Octavian, Lepidus and Antony remembered this precedent, when they gained control of Italy in 43 BC.

Sulla now aimed to abolish all the constitutional change that had been made since the laws of the Gracchi. His intention was to safeguard the role of the Senate as the ruling body of Rome. He took on the position of dictator, which was a traditional Roman office whereby an individual could be granted absolute power without judicial review for a period of six months to meet a dire emergency. In fact, Sulla's dictatorship lasted for almost two years, until he resigned office in 79 BC. During this period he passed a number of laws designed to reinforce the position of the Senate. He handed control of the law courts back to senators, which gave greater security to provincial governors. He increased the number of quaestors (junior magistrates elected each year) from 12 to 20. Quaestors then became senators for life and this helped to guarantee the size of the Senate. Most importantly, he weakened the authority of the tribunes. He took away their most important powers and made them ineligible for any higher magistracy. This ensured that ambitious young men avoided this position and so it became more of a ceremonial role. Sulla also established strict age limits for political office.

The major difficulty that Sulla faced was to abolish his own example. His career had made clear that ultimate power lay in the hands of whoever controlled the legions. Neither Julius Caesar nor Augustus neglected this lesson. Sulla gave the Senate the power to determine which former magistrate would govern each province. He also passed a treason law that forbade a governor to make war without the Senate's initiative or to leave his province without permission. These laws became the bedrock of the political beliefs held by the *optimates* in the late republic. However, after Sulla's retirement in 79 BC and his death the next year, ambitious men soon challenged his political settlement. The years between Sulla's death and the accession of Augustus are probably the best known in Roman history. Our literary sources are extensive and this period is full of important personalities. The next 30 years witnessed the political rivalry of powerful military commanders, ending with a major civil war fought throughout the republic between the supporters of Pompey and Caesar.

Pompey had raised an army in support of Sulla when he invaded Italy and he proved to be one of his most successful commanders in the war against the Marians. He sought to maintain his powerful position by achieving a series of military commands. In 70 BC he was elected consul despite being below Sulla's minimum age limit. Crassus, another powerful supporter of Sulla, was his colleague. Pompey and Crassus changed the composition of the Roman courts to end the monopoly of senators on the juries and to give the *equites* an important role. They also restored the rights of the tribunes that Sulla had abolished. This reform made both of them more popular with the citizens in Rome. More importantly it also enabled Pompey to use the tribunes to propose that he should receive yet more military commands. These extraordinary commands created a precedent for the Senate to grant Augustus control over a large number of provinces after 27 BC.

In 67 BC the tribune Gabinius proposed that Pompey should be empowered to wipe out the pirates who had caused havoc in the Eastern Mediterranean from their bases in Cilicia (southern Turkey) and who had done great damage to the interests of Roman businessmen. Initially this was very unpopular in the Senate, but Pompey was spectacularly successful in organising powerful military forces and capturing and killing large number of pirates. Pompey's popularity increased yet further, and he followed up his success by arranging for the tribune Manilius to propose that he should be given the command against King Mithridates, who had threatened the Romans in the east for the previous 20 years. Another Roman general, Lucullus, who like Pompey had been a prominent supporter of Sulla, had been in overall command in this war for some time. He had won significant victories but was unable to finish the war outright. Pompey was able to arrange for reinforcements and finally succeed in trapping Mithridates, who committed suicide in 63 BC. Pompey then reorganised the lands of the Eastern Mediterranean, adding the new provinces of Cilicia and Syria to the Roman territories.

Pompey returned to Rome with his army with the intention of celebrating a triumph. Unlike Sulla, he had no intention of using his army to eliminate his opponents. Pompey tended to build alliances with either the *populares* or the *optimates*, depending on which group would support his interests at the time. His main aims were simply to be acknowledged as the leading man in Rome and for his authority to be sufficient to implement his wishes. Initially his two priorities were for the Senate to grant land for his veteran troops and for it to ratify his settlement in the east. However, Lucullus was furious at his replacement and he had influential friends. A number of senators believed that Pompey was too anxious to claim credit for achievements based on the work of others. Thus Pompey was frustrated in his attempts to secure his aims and became prepared to consider more radical methods to preserve his reputation.

The years from 70 BC to 62 BC saw the rise to prominence of the famous Roman politician and writer, Marcus Tullius Cicero. Cicero's speeches and letters are our most significant historical source for political events from 63 BC to 43 BC and he was particularly important in Octavian's introduction to the bear-pit of Roman public life. As praetor Cicero had supported Pompey's command against Mithridates and had been elected consul for 63 BC despite being a *novus homo*. As consul he uncovered and put down the conspiracy of Catiline. Catiline had been one of his defeated rivals for the consulship, and after a further electoral failure he had plotted to assassinate Cicero and to take over the state by force. Cicero uncovered these plans and denounced Catiline as a traitor to his face in front of the Senate (Cicero, *Catiline Orations*, I). When Catiline fled to join his armed supporters north of Rome, Cicero had rounded up five of his senatorial accomplices—including Lentulus, one of the praetors—and with the support of the Senate ordered them to be executed without trial. Catiline and his remaining followers were defeated in a battle in northern Italy by an army under the authority of Cicero's colleague as consul, Gaius Antonius. Catiline himself was killed in the battle, along with most of his men.

Initially Cicero's actions made him widely popular in Rome, not only among the senators but also among the poorer citizens. Catiline had been the darling of the Roman mob, but he lost all his popularity because of his attempts to gain the help of the Allobroges, a Gallic tribe beyond Rome's borders, and because he had freed slaves to join his forces. However, the tribune Clodius prosecuted Cicero for these actions before the Roman assembly in 58 BC. Cicero had to endure a humiliating period of exile, before his recall in August 57 BC. Undoubtedly Cicero had shown courage and ability in defying Catiline; he showed the same courage as an old man in 43BC in his final defence of the republic.

Gaius Julius Caesar is an even more important figure who rose to prominence during these years. He was born in 100 BC into an ancient patrician family who claimed descent from Aeneas the Trojan, and thus from Venus, goddess of love. However, the Julii had not enjoyed political success in the previous century. In order to try and recover their fortunes, Caesar's aunt had married Gaius Marius, and this connection led to Caesar following the *popularis* path from an early age. After the coup of Marius and Cinna, the young Julius Caesar married Cinna's daughter, who was also patrician, and thus of the highest social rank in Rome.

When Sulla had returned to power in 82 BC he ordered Caesar to divorce his young wife, but he had refused. This action was an early sign of Julius Caesar's courage, as most of those who defied Sulla were quickly eliminated. Caesar soon fled the city but he was fortunate in having connections from his mother's family, the Aurelii, who were close to Sulla and persuaded the dictator to spare Caesar's life. Sulla is supposed to have said, 'I see many Gaius Mariuses in this young man' (Suetonius, *The Twelve Caesars*, Julius Caesar, 1), but this does rather seem like a quote invented with the benefit of hindsight.

Julius Caesar made his first important mark on Roman political life in 63 BC, when he was elected by the Roman people as *pontifex maximus* (chief priest in Rome), ahead of two much more senior opponents. Caesar intended this to be the first step of a dramatic political career. His link with the Marian cause and his natural political gifts ensured that he was very popular with both the poorer citizens and with the *equites*, and he enjoyed spectacular success in free elections. He served as praetor for 62 BC and then went to the province of Further Spain as governor. On his return in 60 BC he aimed to be elected consul in 59 BC but was well aware that his opponents among the *optimates* would try as far as possible to prevent his election. Since Caesar's popularity meant that they were unlikely to achieve this, however, they would do everything they could to make sure that he achieved nothing as consul.

Caesar's response to this difficult position was to devise a bold and complex political strategy. When Pompey returned victorious he failed to achieve his political objectives; Lucullus and his other *optimate* opponents had prevented him from confirming his settlement of the Roman provinces in the east and they had stopped him from gaining grants of sufficient land to settle his veterans. These two failures represented a grave blow to Pompey's *dignitas*. He had initially wanted to work together with the senatorial oligarchy but they were too wary of his personal ambition. Thus Pompey was prepared to cooperate with the notorious Caesar, provided that Caesar could deliver Pompey's agenda.

Crassus was the second most powerful man in Rome after Pompey. He and Pompey had been rivals ever since their shared consulship of 70 BC. Crassus had supported Caesar's rise through the political ranks and by 60 BC he wanted to secure more direct personal influence. He had promised the *publicani*, a tax-collecting syndicate, that he would secure them a rebate after they had over-estimated the possible profit from the province of Asia (western Turkey). Crassus needed Caesar's support to secure this measure and he was prepared to work with his rival Pompey in order to achieve this.

Thus Caesar created the political alliance known as the first triumvirate, which was to determine the course of political events for the next ten years. We learn from one of Cicero's letters that he rejected an approach from Caesar to support this alliance (*Letters to Atticus*, II.18). Caesar was elected as the senior consul for 59 BC but his colleague was the arch-*optimate* Bibulus, who vowed to prevent Caesar from causing any damage to Rome's constitution. At the beginning of 59 BC, Caesar married his daughter Julia to Pompey. Despite the age difference (Julia was 18 and Pompey was 46), this marriage was successful and—so long as it lasted—it helped to preserve *amicitia* (political friendship) between Pompey and Caesar. Political marriage was an important factor behind alliances between powerful families in Rome, and Augustus extended this tradition with his arrangements for his new royal family.

Caesar's first action as consul in 59 BC was to propose in the Senate a law to find land for Pompey's veterans. The Senate refused to accept this bill, so Caesar took it to the Tribal Assembly. Caesar had learnt the lesson of the Gracchi and made sure that he had overwhelming force on the ground in Rome; he was backed by a number of Pompey's soldiers in the Forum. He then brought in a more radical bill known as the *Lex Campania* that redistributed some of the best public land in Italy to veterans and poorer citizens. Bibulus tried to obstruct all of Caesar's measures, but he was forced to withdraw by the city mob. Bibulus then threatened to have Caesar prosecuted for passing his laws by violence, which meant that Caesar had to watch his position carefully over the next few years. He was immune from prosecution as consul and he retained his immunity when he was appointed proconsul to govern the provinces of Illyricum and Cisalpine Gaul after a vote in the Tribal Assembly proposed by the tribune Vatinius. A later vote in the same assembly added the further province of Transalpine Gaul to Caesar's command after the death of the previous governor. Caesar knew that if he reverted to being a private citizen he was very likely to be prosecuted and that this would result in him losing all of his power and status.

Caesar had displayed some of his military talent during his year as governor of Further Spain and he was desperate to gain command of a major army. This ambition explains the risks he was prepared to run as consul in 59 BC. From 58 BC to 52 BC Julius Caesar won a series of dramatic victories over the Gallic tribes, culminating in his decisive defeat of the Gallic revolt in 52 BC at the battle of Alesia. These victories extended Rome's territory in the west and transformed Caesar's political position. He gained great wealth that enabled him to increase his political influence in Rome. He also became even more popular with the Roman public. On the other hand, the *optimates* feared him even more. Influential senators such as Cato were prepared to compromise with Pompey in order to have the opportunity to crush Caesar.

As a result, Pompey and Caesar gradually drifted apart. When Cicero returned from exile he attempted to persuade Pompey to move away from Caesar and attacked the *Lex Campania*. His strategy initially failed because Caesar brought Pompey and Crassus together at the conference at Luca in his province in Cisalpine Gaul. They were accompanied by 120 senators to act as the supporters of the three principal leaders. Caesar put together a deal that was too good for Pompey and Crassus to turn down. Caesar himself was to receive five more years of command in Gaul; Pompey and Crassus were to stand as consuls for 55 BC and then were to receive their own special military commands. Crassus received the chance to equal the military glory of Pompey and Caesar, and was appointed as governor of Syria and given a large force to attack the Parthian Empire. Pompey was to receive command over both provinces in Spain. However, he was granted the right to administer these provinces through two legates under his personal command; he himself would remain in Rome to establish order there.

Initially these arrangements worked out well for Caesar. Pompey ordered Cicero to stop attacking Caesar's legislation, and Cicero finally abandoned his attempt to follow an independent political line and buckled down to support the triumvirate. However, the bonds that held Caesar and Pompey together gradually loosened. In 54 BC Pompey's wife Julia died in childbirth. Pompey was stricken with grief, but rejected an offer to renew the alliance by marrying another female relative of Caesar and instead married Cornelia, the daughter of a leading *optimate*, Metellus Scipio. From then on he progressively moved closer to Caesar's *optimate* opponents. The next year Crassus' attempt to build a reputation to match his colleagues met with disaster. The

Parthians ambushed his invasion force and wiped them out at the battle of Carrhae in 53 BC. Crassus himself was killed and his head was thrown at the feet of the Parthian king. The Parthians also captured a number of legionary battle standards, known as *aquilae* (eagles). Augustus eventually managed to retrieve these important symbols of Roman honour by diplomacy many years later. If Crassus had been successful in the east, Pompey would not have been strong enough to take on both of his rivals. Now the *optimates* believed that they had the opportunity to dismiss Caesar from command of his province and then to prosecute him for his actions as consul in 59 BC.

Caesar was well aware that his opponents wanted to attack him and he came up with a plan to preserve his position. In 52 BC a bill sponsored by all ten tribunes had granted him the right to stand for the consulship without attending Rome. Caesar hoped to be elected as the consul for 48 BC and then to move on to take command against the Parthians. All the time his immunity would be preserved. At this crucial stage in his career Caesar displayed a mastery of propaganda. He published his *Gallic Wars* that described his wonderful victories and which still survive today. These eloquent accounts of his military actions improved his popularity in Rome and made his opponents more afraid of his powerful army. Augustus shared Caesar's talent for promoting his own image and used both writers and architects to publicise his achievements.

The move towards civil war began in 51 BC. One of the consuls for that year, Marcus Marcellus, was a passionate opponent of Caesar and attempted to have him recalled from Gaul. Caesar had now crushed the Gallic opposition and the situation was calm enough for him to be replaced by another governor. Marcellus persuaded the Senate to agree to discuss a possible successor for Caesar on 1 March 50 BC. However, Caesar was determined not to give up his immunity as to do so would allow his opponents to prosecute him in front of a picked jury. He managed to secure the support of a talented young tribune called Gaius Scribonius Curio. This was a great surprise for the Senate, as Curio had previously been a promising young *optimate*. Caesar had agreed to pay all of Curio's debts and received loyal service in return.

Curio vetoed any discussion of a replacement for Caesar throughout 50 BC. Instead, he made a series of peace proposals on Caesar's behalf. Curio suggested that both Caesar and Pompey should give up their commands. Pompey had renewed his command over Spain for five years in 52 BC, so they were not in the same legal position. This proposal made Caesar appear anxious for compromise, and helped swing public opinion in his favour. Pompey now finally put himself clearly on the *optimate* side and made a counter-proposal that Caesar should leave his province on 13 November 50 BC. Curio again vetoed this and on 1 December put to the Senate his proposal that both Pompey and Caesar should give up their commands. Such was the longing for peace that this proposal was carried by 370 votes to 22.

However, it was Caesar's opponents who had the clearest sense of purpose. Gaius Marcellus, one of the two consuls, dismissed the Senate and symbolically offered Pompey a sword to defend the freedom of Italy. Pompey accepted the sword and committed himself to leading the armed opposition to Caesar. Curio's term of office ended towards the end of 50 BC but Marcus Antonius (better known as Mark Antony), a loyal supporter of Caesar, had been elected tribune for 49 BC and he continued to veto any attempt to dismiss Caesar. Despite this, the new consuls for 49 BC were determined to force a confrontation. Antony fled from Rome to Ravenna in Cisalpine Gaul, Caesar's southern province, claiming that his life was in danger. This gave Caesar an additional cause for declaring war on the Senate. His main appeal to his men was based on his personal honour. His *dignitas* was being violated; despite all his victories, he was to be condemned and disgraced. His men were unlikely to receive any reward for all their years of hard fighting. He now appealed to his constituency in Rome by proclaiming that he was fighting to preserve the rights of tribunes and the liberty of the Roman people. His military calculations were combined with his sense of public opinion.

Nevertheless, Julius Caesar's decision to cross the river Rubicon and begin the civil war was an outrageous gamble. Gaius Octavius, aged 14, would have been old enough to grasp the gravity of the situation and to understand the importance for his own future as a member of the same family. Caesar was following Sulla's example by marching on Rome to defend his own political position. His swift advance took his opponents by surprise and they were unable to mount an effective resistance in Italy. Pompey sensibly retreated to Greece in order to recruit military forces from his vast *clientela* in the eastern provinces. Only Domitius Ahenobarbus, consul in 54 BC, attempted to resist Caesar at the town of Corfinium. Caesar surrounded him and seduced his troops into mutiny by appealing directly to Ahenobarbus' soldiers. Once he was in control of Italy, Caesar took on the republican office of dictator to justify his authority, just as Sulla had done. His policy towards his defeated opponents sharply diverged from Sulla's: instead of exterminating his enemies, he forgave them. His slogan was *clementia* (mercy). This had a powerful effect on public opinion and even an opponent such as Cicero was favourably impressed. This policy continued after Caesar won devastating victories against Pompey's legions; first in Spain, where Caesar describes how he encouraged his soldiers to make contact with former comrades so that he could win over deserters from Pompey's forces (*Civil War*, I.74), and then at the decisive battle of Pharsalus in northern Greece. Pompey himself survived the battle and fled to Egypt, the wealthiest kingdom beyond Rome's borders. Soon after his arrival he was murdered on the orders of the young Egyptian king's advisers, who decided they should back the winning side.

This was the point where many of Caesar's opponents appealed to the mercy of the victor. Leading politicians such as Cicero, Marcus Brutus and Cassius were granted forgiveness and honourable positions in the Senate. However, they were horrified by Caesar's growing autocracy and, despite their personal debt to him, they were forced by their consciences into opposition. In Cicero's case, we know from his letters that his opposition took the form of private grumbling and complaint (*Letters to Atticus*, XIII.40). Marcus Brutus and Cassius took the more dramatic path of plotting Caesar's assassination. Octavian must have drawn the conclusion from this result that *clementia* should have its limits.

The civil war did not end with Pompey's death; Julius Caesar faced more than three years of hard fighting to confirm his victory. The most hard-line *optimates* refused to accept Caesar's *clementia* and rallied their forces in the province of Africa. The leader of this army was Pompey's father-in-law, Metellus Scipio, but Marcus Porcius Cato was the inspiration behind the continuing resistance to Caesar. Cato had been Caesar's most bitter opponent throughout his career, and Cato had instigated the policy of provoking confrontation in 49 BC. He now inspired many of the surviving senators to use their resources to fight on. Caesar's military skill proved too much for this force and he crushed Metellus' army at the battle of Thapsus in north Africa. Rather than submit to Caesar, Cato preferred to commit suicide in the city of Utica, tearing out his own entrails when doctors attempted to save him. Cato's example inspired Caesar's republican opponents and illustrated just how determined the republicans could be.

Pompey's two sons survived the defeat at Thapsus and rallied the republican cause in Spain. The young Gaius Octavius joined Caesar as he again led an army to the province and won his final victory of the civil war at the battle of Munda in March 45 BC. Pompey's eldest son Gaius Pompeius was killed; only Sextus Pompeius survived to be a rival to Octavian in the next generation. The strength of the Pompeian faction and the power of Pompey's name is evident from the fact that it took Caesar four separate campaigns in Spain, Greece, Africa, then Spain again to destroy their resistance and even then Sextus Pompeius was able to put together a naval force in the next decade in the Mediterranean islands of Sardinia and Corsica.

At last Julius Caesar could return to Rome for his triumph. There was simply no one left to fight. He had little time to develop his vision for Rome's future. Although his policy of *clementia* had allowed many of his former opponents to survive, Caesar made little attempt to conciliate them. Cicero's disgruntled letters to his friend Atticus in these years illustrate why Caesar's opponents became so desperate. At the end of 45 BC, on the death of the consul Quintus Fabius Maximus, Caesar allowed one of his supporters, Caninius Rebilus, to be consul for a day. Cicero utilised all his wit to mock the scandal of this situation, but he clearly considered that Caesar was destroying the value of the consulship that Cicero had considered such a prize (*Letters to his Friends*, VII.xxx)

Worse was to follow. In January 44 BC, Caesar assumed the title of *dictator perpetuus* (dictator for life). This violated the constitutional principle that the dictatorship should be granted for a limited period to overcome a crisis. Even Sulla had obeyed this principle by giving up the dictatorship in 80 BC, shortly before his death. Caesar indicated that he was rejecting this example with his quip that Sulla did not know his ABC when he gave up the dictatorship (Suetonius, *The Twelve Caesars*, Julius Caesar, 77). The image that Caesar now created for himself was more provocative and more regal than any Roman had created before. The month of Quinctilis was renamed as Julius—which of course is the origin of our month of July. He ordered that statues of himself should be placed in the temple of Quirinus, near the statues of the kings of Rome. Cicero was outraged by these actions and, although he played no part in the conspiracy to assassinate Caesar, he was delighted by its success.

One famous incident shows how Caesar attempted to define his new image and how his public actions encouraged the conspiracy. The feast of the Lupercalia was celebrated on 15 February 44 BC. The plot to assassinate Caesar had almost certainly already begun, but the events of that day would have helped the leaders to recruit more members. Mark Antony had now risen to the rank of Caesar's fellow consul, and was publicly recognised as one of his closest political friends. Antony took part in the traditional festival of the Luperci, a college of priests who staged a ceremonial run throughout the centre of Rome, wearing only loincloths. At the end of the course, Antony three times offered Caesar a diadem that looked like a crown. Caesar rejected it each time, and then ordered that the jewel should be dedicated at the temple of Jupiter. The official archives recorded that Antony as consul had offered the crown to Caesar as *dictator perpetuus* and that Caesar had declined it.

At first glance, this incident might have served to reduce speculation that Caesar would become king. In fact, our sources indicate the exact opposite. The title *rex* and the idea of monarchy was so outrageous for the Roman upper class that they were horrified that it had even been proposed. It beggars belief that two such adept and experienced manipulators of opinion as Caesar and Antony would have allowed this incident to occur spontaneously. As Cicero points out in a later speech, it seemed odd that Antony was carrying a diadem at all. The event must have been pre-arranged by Caesar and Antony to make a political point. We cannot be sure what the plan was; whether it was to dampen speculation that Caesar intended to become king or whether Antony was testing the water. Certainly the hostile republicans believed the second motive at the time.

Whatever Caesar and Antony's intentions, the consequences were disastrous. Caesar's actions seemed designed to cause maximum provocation but he was making very little attempt to safeguard his own security. Caesar's actions—such as the dismantling of his bodyguard and the anecdotes that he wished for a sudden death (e.g. Suetonius *The Twelve Caesars*, Julius Caesar, 87)—do suggest a certain world-weariness. In contrast, Augustus took great care over his own security and, once in power, he ensured that his autocracy would not offend the political sensibilities of senatorial opinion. Julius Caesar's spectacular career demonstrated that the republic could not control a charismatic and powerful general. Caesar had the audacity to overthrow the existing constitution, yet failed to establish the basis for lasting reform. Augustus rebuilt the Roman state to enable it to survive for another 500 years.

The most famous date in Roman history is 15 March 44 BC, and the events of the Ides of March were the greatest political shock of the time. Just three days before he was due to depart for a major military campaign against the Parthians Julius Caesar was assassinated by a large group of senators, led by Marcus Brutus and Cassius. Cicero quickly moved to support them. The surviving consul Mark Antony attempted to fill the power vacuum and to establish himself quickly as the leader of Caesar's faction. Gaius Octavius, Caesar's great-nephew and closest male relative, heard the dreadful news at the town of Apollonia in Macedonia. He had been preparing to accompany Caesar on his Parthian campaign. Some of his closest relations advised him to reject his inheritance and retire into private life. Instead the 18-year-old decided to head for Italy. It was a decision that changed the world.

PART II

Gaius Julius Caesar Octavianus

CHAPTER 3

CALCULATED RISKS

The young Gaius Octavius was born on 23 September 63 BC in the year of Cicero's consulship, in the town of Velitrae, approximately 20 miles south-east of Rome. His father, also called Gaius Octavius, was from the leading family of that town. Although he had no senatorial ancestors, this older Gaius Octavius entered the Senate as a *novus homo* and served as praetor. He was a successful governor of Macedonia and hoped to stand for the consulship. However, he died at Nola in Central Italy shortly after his return in 58 BC. Thus Augustus would have scarcely been able to remember his father, but his important political connection was through his mother Atia. She was Julius Caesar's niece: the daughter of Caesar's sister, and this made the young Gaius Octavius one of Julius Caesar's three closest male relatives, all of whom were his great-nephews. The evidence of Caesar's will, drawn up in September 45 BC, suggests that Octavius became his favourite: the other two great nephews, Lucius Pinarius and Quintus Pedius, each received one-eighth of Caesar's estate, but Gaius Octavius was adopted in his will and was granted three-quarters of the estate. He also received the name Gaius Julius Caesar Octavianus. The adoption was much more significant than the money since it entitled Octavius to call himself Caesar's son and heir, and enabled him to raise an army in the tumultuous aftermath of Caesar's assassination.

After her husband's death, Atia swiftly remarried a more prominent politician, Lucius Marcus Philippus, who became consul in 56 BC. Philippus provided the young Octavius with useful political support in his early career, but his connection with Caesar was the most important factor from an early stage of his life, as Caesar rose to the top of political life in Rome. In 45 BC, Octavius was elevated to patrician status, making him a member of the highest aristocracy in Rome. This was just the sort of political patronage that the republicans hated. Suetonius also records that Octavius had followed Caesar to Spain for the campaign against Pompey's sons, and joined Caesar's camp after journeying through hostile territory and despite a serious illness (Suetonius, *The Twelve Caesars*, Augustus, 8). There is quite a bit of evidence that Octavius' health was weak in his early years and he may well have suffered from asthma, which improved as he grew older.

Julius Caesar wanted to continue Octavius' political apprenticeship and had arranged for him to sail to Apollonia in Macedonia to join some of the legions that were preparing for the campaign against the Parthians. Caesar intended Octavius to accompany this expedition to boost his profile and to gain further experience. His friend Marcus Agrippa, who was to be his most important associate in his rise to absolute power, accompanied him on this trip. When Octavius heard of Caesar's assassination and the chaos in Rome, he took the fateful decision to return to Brundisium in southern Italy, and he had successfully completed the journey by the end of April. Both hardened Caesarians such as Antony and Lepidus, and determined republicans such as Cassius and Cicero, had left Octavius out of their calculations. In fact, Octavius' return to Italy was the first step in a 14-year journey that would lead him to absolute power in the Roman world.

Octavian (to avoid confusion, I will follow the convention of calling him Octavian from his adoption by Julius Caesar until 27 BC, when he took the name Augustus) displayed great subtlety and total ruthlessness in his unprecedented rise to power in 44 BC and 43 BC. He took some decisive actions soon after his return to Brundisium. Octavian was very fortunate in these early years that he was able to raise large sums of money. The likelihood is that the financiers Balbus and Oppius, and other members of Julius' Caesar's influential staff made the decision to support Octavian at this early stage. Cicero describes the size and power of Caesar's staff when the dictator had paid him a final visit in December 45 BC (*Letters to Atticus*, XIII.52). Balbus had conducted his accounts with Caesar in the morning and Cicero had needed three dining rooms to entertain Caesar's entourage before enduring a strained discussion about literature. These two men, both obsessed with politics, had not been able to find any common ground in their discussion of the republic. Mark Antony and other Caesarian leaders would have taken over some of Caesar's staff, but the evidence suggests that many of these well-informed and wealthy *equites* and freedmen put their considerable weight behind Octavian.

One explanation for why the young man seems to have been so politically adept from such a young age could be that he was well advised by experienced figures such as Balbus and Oppius. If so, Octavian certainly deserves great credit for following this advice so successfully. Balbus was well rewarded for his support and became consul in 40 BC. Octavian was also supported by a talented group of personal friends: Agrippa became a great military commander, while Maecenas became the most famous diplomat and political adviser in Octavian's circle. Octavian later wrote an autobiography describing his achievements up to 27 BC and dedicated it to Agrippa and Maecenas. Sadly this autobiography does not survive, but it is likely to have been the main source for other historians such as Nicolaus of Damascus and Velleius Paterculus, whose works have come through to us.

It is worth considering why Octavian took the risk of not merely claiming the personal inheritance of his great-uncle, but also proclaiming himself to be the political heir of Julius Caesar. Both his mother and his stepfather advised Octavian to decline Caesar's inheritance as too great a risk. He would earn the hostility of ideological republicans such as Marcus Brutus and Cassius, and he would also be in danger from Caesarian leaders such as Mark Antony, who was bitter that he had not been named as Caesar's heir since he was his most prominent supporter and also a blood relation. However, Octavian must have calculated that inaction would almost certainly have proved dangerous as well. As the heir to Caesar's fortune and his name he could have been the target for retribution from either side. Perhaps Octavian calculated that his best hope to secure his personal safety was to place himself at the head of Caesar's legions.

Octavian immediately gained control of the military treasury that had been left in Brundisium for the Parthian campaign. The legions based in the area greeted him enthusiastically when he declared himself to be Gaius Julius Caesar. Adoption was a common custom in Rome in this period and the legionaries made little distinction between an adopted and a natural son. It was natural for the soldiers who had loved Julius Caesar to serve his son. No other leader could match the magic of this name. By the time Octavian reached Rome in May, he was the leader of an army and a man to be reckoned with. The leader to whom he presented the greatest challenge was in fact Mark Antony, and Antony immediately treated him as a threat.

Antony had played a clever hand in the aftermath of Caesar's assassination. He must have initially feared for his own personal safety, and Cicero was repeatedly to criticise the conspirators for not killing Antony and some other leading Caesarians as well. He later described the Ides of March as 'a wonderful feast, but only half-complete' and said that 'If I had been in charge, there would have been no leftovers' (*Letters to his Friends*, X.28, etc.). However, Marcus Brutus saw the murder of Caesar as a form of ritual sacrifice and insisted that no one else should be killed to preserve the honour of the assassins.

Antony was initially conciliatory towards the conspirators and the republican faction. The Senate agreed an amnesty for the assassins, who called themselves the 'Liberators', but Caesar's acts were declared legal, which safeguarded Antony's position as consul. Antony's next move was to fire up the crowd with a rousing speech at Caesar's funeral (Suetonius, *The Twelve Caesars*, *Julius Caesar*, 84; Appian, *Civil Wars*, II.144). He was helped by the provisions of Caesar's will in which the dictator had bequeathed 75 denarii to every male citizen in Rome. Caesar had continued to be very popular among the urban poor, and there was a strong constituency prepared to support anyone who would make a stand to avenge his death and stand up for the rights of the poorer citizens of the city. Riots broke out and Marcus Brutus and Cassius were forced to flee from Rome. Cicero too was very anxious for his own safety and stayed out of Rome until September.

Once he was established in Rome, Octavian showed himself to be a skilful agitator. He criticised Antony for not acting firmly enough in support of Caesar. He invoked the traditional Roman virtue of *pietas* by demanding vengeance for his father and by paying out the sums from Caesar's will when Antony was slow in making the payment. Balbus and Oppius' fund-raising abilities must have been crucial in helping him to carry out this pledge. A comet appeared while Octavian was celebrating Caesar's funeral games in July and he declared that this was proof that Julius Caesar should be worshipped as a god. In the autumn of 44 BC two of Antony's legions based near Brundisium mutinied and joined Octavian. The likelihood is that this was because Octavian had offered them higher pay as well as the magical name of Caesar. Octavian now had popular support and significant military backing, but he now needed some way of establishing his legitimacy and he achieved this through a political manoeuvre that astonished his contemporaries.

Antony's response to Octavian's intervention had been to secure a law in the Tribal Assembly to give him control of the provinces of Cisalpine and Transalpine Gaul at the end of his consulship. This would give Antony strategic control over Italy from the north, but did not necessarily commit him to unconstitutional action. However, one of the leading assassins of Caesar, Decimus Junius Brutus, was the existing governor of Cisalpine Gaul and he refused to give up his position. He also controlled a significant number of legions and prepared to withstand a siege at the town of Mutina. In spite of this, Antony's victory appeared inevitable because he led a large army of experienced Caesarian veterans.

The one thing that prevented Antony from defeating Decimus Brutus without difficulty was the power of the oratory of Cicero. Cicero had returned to Rome at the end of August 44 BC and made a series of speeches in the Senate denouncing Antony and calling him a traitor to the republic. These speeches still survive, and are known as the *Philippics*. The confrontation between Cicero and Antony grew more and more bitter as the year went on, and each of them used more provocative language about the other. As mentioned above, Cicero had been acknowledged as Rome's leading orator since his prosecution of Verres over 25 years earlier, and his speeches had a dramatic effort on public opinion and on the beliefs of the senators. Most of the old *optimate* senators had died fighting Julius Caesar at Pharsalus, Thapsus or Munda, but the power of the orator worked even on senators who had been appointed by Caesar, and Cicero succeeded in cobbling together an effective coalition to oppose Antony from moderate Caesarians and surviving republicans. He did not achieve this simply through great oratory: we have a significant number of the letters Cicero sent appealing for support and trying to bolster his position (e.g. *Letters to his Friends*, X.6 and X.28). He was well aware of the difficulties of his position. In one of his letters to Atticus he sums up his situation by saying, 'We are desperate for men and money, but have little hope of either.' (*Letters to Atticus*, XIV.4) His apparently hopeless situation prompted him into an unexpected move.

Octavian commanded a significant number of troops and had the money to pay for them. He was also no friend of Antony. Thus he decided to approach Cicero to propose an alliance. However, Octavian had raised his troops on the promise of avenging Caesar, and now he was cooperating with Caesar's opponent Cicero and potentially his assassin Decimus Brutus against Caesar's right-hand man Mark Antony. It says much for Octavian's powers of persuasion that his troops were prepared to follow him north to march against their former comrades. Perhaps they had some idea that Octavian was not firmly committed to this new alliance.

Cicero's letters to his friend Atticus provide a fascinating insight into Octavian's entry to the world of Roman politics (e.g. *Letters to Atticus*, XV.11 and XV.12). On 31 October 44 BC Octavian sent a letter to Cicero, offering to make an alliance with the republicans against Antony. At first Cicero was sceptical, but Octavian persisted in his approaches to him. Cicero records on 4 November that he received two letters from Octavian on the same day (*Letters to Atticus*, XVI.15). The tone of these letters was impeccably deferential to Rome's senior statesman, and Cicero was obviously flattered by the approach. He conceived the hope that he might be able to influence this charming young man and convert him to the cause of the republic. He was also well aware that the republicans did not have the troops or the money to challenge Antony in Italy.

Meanwhile, Octavian led his first march on Rome with 3,000 troops to appeal to the Roman people. Just like Julius Caesar and Sulla, he showed no compunction in breaking the sacred convention about bringing troops within the city boundaries of Rome, the *pomerium*. His public rhetoric was still unashamedly Caesarian and he vowed to continue to follow his father's example. In private he continued negotiations with both moderate Caesarians such as the designated consuls for 43 BC, Aulus Hirtius and Gaius Vibius Pansa Caetronianus, and with republicans such as Cicero. His strategy did not meet with immediate success. Antony also led his troops inside the *pomerium*, and called a Senate meeting with the intention of indicting Octavian for treason. He was prevented from doing so by the risk of mutiny among his men; Octavian's agents were doing effective work, calling on the former soldiers of Caesar to support his son, and promising higher pay. In the struggle for power in the civil wars between 44 BC and 30 BC Octavian's most effective weapon was often his ability to incite mutiny in the enemy camp. The legions of Octavian and Antony were reluctant to fight each other. Antony blinked first and abandoned his post as consul a month early to march north with four legions to fight with Decimus Brutus in Cisalpine Gaul. His soldiers, ever loyal to the memory of Julius Caesar, were much more content to attack one of his assassins rather than his adopted son.

Cicero's last letter to Atticus on 9 December 44 BC shows that he was continuing to deliberate about the wisdom of forming an alliance with the young Octavian (*Letters to Atticus*, XVI.15). He was greatly deterred by Octavian's speech in honour of Julius Caesar, but delighted that Octavian had got the better of Antony. Cicero talks about how Julius Caesar's former agent Oppius was lobbying him to make an alliance with Octavian. This is fascinating evidence to support the theory that central figures from Julius Caesar's private staff quickly switched their loyalty to Octavian. Cicero responded rather pompously that he would not make an alliance with Octavian until he was convinced he was a friend of Marcus Brutus and Cassius. This condition was clearly impossible, but Oppius continued to use his powers of persuasion, and wore the old orator down.

At the beginning of 43 BC the two new consuls, Hirtius and Pansa, took office. The first important question for the Senate to decide was whether Antony's attempt to control Cisalpine Gaul should be resisted. Cicero entered the debate with a crucial speech, which still survives as the *Third Philippic*. He denounced Antony as an enemy of the Roman state—the same phrase he had used to indict Catiline and his supporters. In later speeches he specifically compared Antony to Catiline, and even more offensively to Spartacus (the leader of the slave rebellion 73–71 BC) (*Phillipics*, IV.6). Cicero made the crucial decision to advocate that Octavian's position as the leader of an army should be legalised, and referred to him respectfully as Caesar. Cicero was effective in persuading the Senate, not because they were enthusiastic republicans, but through the force of his personality and because they were afraid of Antony's potential use of force. On Cicero's proposal, Octavian was appointed a member of the Senate despite his youth, and was granted *imperium* (official command) over his troops, which he placed at the disposal of the Senate for their campaign against Antony. He was granted authority as if he was eligible for military command after serving as a praetor. Thus Octavian's official political career began on 7 January 43 BC, a date he later marked with an official sacrifice. He continued to hold *imperium* for 57 years.

The three armies of Hirtius, Pansa and Octavian marched north to engage Antony. Octavian had reversed his political position from being the most radical advocate of revenge for Caesar's death to being the loyal servant of the republic. It says much for the loyalty of his troops that they continued to follow him, but they remained well paid and they must have retained the faith that Octavian would continue to look after their interests. This faith was certainly justified by subsequent events.

Antony's position had been dramatically weakened over the previous six months, and Cicero's political strategy appeared to be vindicated. Antony had expected to defeat Decimus Brutus' forces without much difficulty. Now he was faced with three more armies, including a number of Caesarian veterans. Antony made the decision to take on these armies one by one, and on 14 April 43 BC he launched an attack on Pansa, whom he thought was leading four newly recruited legions (approximately 20,000 men). In fact Hirtius moved swiftly to support his colleague, and Antony's surprise attack was beaten off, but not before Pansa himself was critically wounded. Hirtius had been a close follower of Julius Caesar and is credited by some historians with having acted as Caesar's ghostwriter for his histories of the Gallic and civil wars. A week later Hirtius showed that his talents were not simply confined to war reporting by organising an effective attack against Antony's forces, coordinating his assault with Decimus Brutus, who launched a sortie from the town of Mutina. Hirtius may well have had doubts about the loyalty of Octavian's forces, which he kept in reserve. Octavian must have been delighted with this decision; he did not need to order his troops into combat against Antony, which might have been difficult since many of the men would have regarded Antony as a comrade from their campaigns with Julius Caesar. Hirtius' plan for the second battle at Mutina was successful and he broke Antony's siege. Antony was forced to move north in the hope that Lepidus, a former subordinate of Julius Caesar, would support him. Lepidus had made overtures to both sides and was likely to support whoever he thought was going to emerge as the winner. Thus Antony was far from assured of a welcome from him after his defeat. It appeared that Cicero's complex web of alliances had defeated the threat from Antony.

However, Hirtius, the hero of Mutina, was killed in the second battle at the moment of victory. Shortly afterwards, Pansa also died from the wounds he had received in the first battle. Casualties had been high, and the consuls' legions were eager to attach themselves to a strong leader. There were two alternatives on the spot, completely hostile to each other, despite the fact that they had been on the same side in the recent battles. It was one thing for Octavian to cooperate with moderate Caesarians such as Hirtius and Pansa against his personal enemy Antony. It was quite another to work together with Decimus Brutus, who was considered the most treacherous of the assassins of Julius Caesar. Cassius and Marcus Brutus had been former supporters of Pompey. Decimus Brutus had fought with Julius Caesar in Gaul and in the civil wars. Caesar had designated him as the consul for 42 BC, so it is unlikely that he had joined the assassins because of lack of rewards. Rather he must have been so opposed to Caesar's autocratic style of leadership that he felt that it would not be worth being consul unless Caesar was removed. The career of Decimus Brutus shows that Caesar had alienated even his own supporters. Augustus was very careful to avoid this mistake when he became the ruler of Rome.

Octavian took immediate and decisive steps to increase his own military strength. He swiftly took command of Hirtius and Pansa's surviving men, and now stood at the head of eight legions. The deaths of Hirtius and Pansa were very convenient for Octavian, and by the time of Tacitus and Suetonius, writing in the next century, there was already speculation that he had organised their murder (Tacitus, *Annals*, I.9; Suetonius, *The Twelve Caesars*, Augustus, 11). Certainly he was capable of such drastic action, but no convincing evidence has been produced to convict him. Octavian now had the power to make his own decisions and refused to cooperate with Decimus Brutus. This left Antony able to escape from any pursuit, even with a terribly weakened army.

When the optimistic news came back to Rome of the success of the Senate's forces, euphoria broke out and led to weak decisions. The Senate hailed the slain consuls as heroes and awarded Decimus Brutus a triumph. There was little attempt to reward Octavian, even though his support was now crucial if Antony was to be defeated. Cicero proposed that Octavian should be granted an ovation (a military award that was inferior in prestige to a triumph) but even this proposal placed him as subordinate to Decimus Brutus. The Senate also proposed to reduce the bounties promised to the victorious legions and left both Decimus Brutus and Octavian off the commission designed to organise this.

A fascinating letter written by Decimus Brutus to Cicero on 24 May 43 BC is crucial for interpreting the state of the relationship between Octavian and Cicero (*Letters to his Friends*, XI.20). In it, Decimus Brutus warns Cicero that someone had spread a rumour that Cicero had made a joke about Octavian, saying the young man must be praised, honoured and 'kicked upstairs'. The crucial Latin word is *tollendum*, which can carry the double meaning of praised or got rid of. The joke is excellent, but hardly appropriate to the desperate situation. Cicero's wit had been getting him into trouble for years; we can not be sure if Cicero did say this, or if Segulius Labeo, who was working on Octavian's staff, invented the remark (as Decimus Brutus suggests in the letter). Certainly the rumour was credible, and Octavian's response, as reported to Decimus Brutus, is instructive. He replied that there was no way that he was going to allow this to happen. Decimus Brutus' letter also warns Cicero that many of those surrounding Octavian were stirring him up against Cicero and that Cicero should not be sure of Octavian's loyalty to the republican cause. He also points out how provocative the Senate's decision was to exclude himself and Octavian from the Commission of Ten, proposed to organise bounties for the victorious troops. The tone of Decimus Brutus' correspondence with Cicero becomes increasingly desperate as they both realised that their chances of victory or even survival were slipping away.

By June 43 BC it was clear that Cicero could not rely on Octavian's loyalty. Antony gathered together his forces after his defeat at Mutina, and forged an alliance with the commanders of the northern and western provinces: Marcus Aemilius Lepidus, Lucius Munatius Plancus and Gaius Asinius Pollio. As Julius Caesar had appointed them all as provincial governors, it was natural that they should cooperate with each other. Antony now commanded the strongest force in the west. In desperation, Decimus Brutus abandoned his troops, who were on the verge of mutiny, and tried to flee to join the strong forces of Marcus Brutus and Cassius in the east. He was captured and executed by a Gallic chief who supported Mark Antony.

Octavian was now clearly acting in his own interests. Cicero announced to the Senate in his *Philippics* that Antony had written to Octavian and had compared Cicero to a *lanista* (a gladiator trainer) who was playing the Caesarians off against themselves for his own purposes. This accusation must have been very believable after the Senate's lack of respect and the rumour of Cicero's black humour at Octavian's expense. Octavian thus made the decision to change sides again, but he knew that he needed to strengthen his position before entering into detailed negotiations with Antony and Lepidus. Marcus Brutus and Cassius had established strong forces in the east of the empire, and the Senate had given legal recognition to the position of Marcus Brutus as governor of Macedonia, and Cassius as governor of Syria. Antony would certainly welcome the help of Octavian and his eight legions to fight this group of republicans. This gave both men sufficient motivation to come to terms.

Thus in August 43 BC Octavian ordered his second march on Rome in less than a year. This time there were no military forces to resist him. A delegation of his centurions demanded that Octavian should be made consul, that they should receive their bounties in full and that the declaration of Antony as a public enemy should be repealed. When a republican senator tried to resist, one of the centurions raised his sword and replied that if the Senate did not make Octavian consul, then his sword would. On 19 August Octavian was elected consul along with his uncle, Quintus Pedius. He was the youngest consul in the history of the republic. With no need to conciliate the republicans, he returned to his populist policy of representing himself as the avenger of Julius Caesar. He ordered that there should be a special tribunal for Caesar's assassins, and he took money from the state treasury to pay a bounty to his veterans. He was now ready for the difficult negotiations with Antony. Marcus Brutus had warned Cicero that his policy of collaboration with Octavian could only lead to disaster (*Letters to Brutus*, XXV). Cicero was devastated that his policies had failed. The last surviving written words of the greatest and most prolific Roman prose writer are a short letter to Octavian thanking him for allowing him not to attend the Senate (*Ad Caesarem Iuniorem* (frag)). Cicero had only four more months to live.

Once Octavian had established his position in Rome, he led his forces north to begin the negotiations with Antony and Lepidus to reunite the Caesarian forces. They now planned a campaign of vengeance against Marcus Brutus and Cassius in the east. The three leaders met near Bologna in Italy, and conducted a secret council of war. Their first decision was to proclaim themselves as triumvirs and joint dictators of the state. Whereas the so-called first triumvirate of Pompey, Crassus and Caesar was a secret political alliance, this second triumvirate was publicly declared and eventually ratified in Rome by an assembly of the people. Of course, the three warlords made sure that this assembly was conducted on their own terms. They preserved the outward forms of legality as much as possible, but made sure that they kept control of all the real levers of power. Under their constitutional settlement their decisions had the force of law, so debate was impossible.

The triumvirate was in effect a council of war, and the three leaders decided that Antony and Octavian would lead an aggressive military campaign against Marcus Brutus and Cassius. Lepidus would safeguard their control of the western half of the empire. In order to wage this war effectively, the triumvirs would need to eliminate any prospect of opposition and they needed to raise as much money as possible to pay for their troops. They decided to achieve these aims by following the example of Sulla. Caesar's assassination had proved the risks of *clementia*. The triumvirs were determined to wage total war and prepared to use the utmost brutality. Thus they drew up death lists, using the same euphemism of proscriptions employed by Sulla. They put both political opponents and men of property on the list and organised death squads to kill their opponents and acquire their wealth.

The Cicero family headed the list of illustrious victims. Later apologists for Octavian claimed that he tried to save Cicero, but Antony was determined to eliminate his most bitter enemy. Generations of admirers of Cicero have condemned Antony for ordering the murder of their hero, but one has to remember that Cicero, great man of letters that he was, had repeatedly called for the assassination of Antony. First Cicero's brother and nephew were killed and then Cicero himself was ambushed by a troop of Antony's soldiers while attempting a half-hearted escape. Plutarch's description of the death of Cicero is one of the most famous passages in ancient history. Cicero was reading Euripides' *Medea*. When he realised that he was surrounded, he ordered his slaves not to resist, stuck out his neck and told the leader of the soldier to kill him quickly. Plutarch describes him dying in a similar fashion to the gladiators he had admired in his writings (Plutarch, *Cicero*, XLVII).

The numbers killed in these proscriptions were appalling to contemporaries. One source estimated that 300 senators were killed and 2,000 *equites*. Combined with the casualties in the civil wars, this meant that there was dramatic change in the membership of the upper class. The republican spirit that had motivated men such as Cato and Cicero no longer survived. As the wars continued, the few surviving aristocrats such as Marcus Valerius Messala and the most eloquent poets such as Virgil and Horace eventually became advocates of a new state, which could at least preserve peace and allow men of property to enjoy the delights of private life.

Octavian spent the next year consolidating his control over his legions and preparing for the war against Marcus Brutus and Cassius. His relationship with Antony would always be tense, but they were now publicly united in the cause of defeating the assassins of Caesar. Veteran troops of both leaders were much more content as they had been well paid, and were now directed to a popular cause. The triumvirs made a clear public statement of their loyalty to Julius Caesar's legacy. They ordered the building of a temple to Divus Julius, the deified Julius Caesar, in the Roman Forum and ordered that his cult should be celebrated in the towns of Italy.

However, Marcus Brutus and Cassius had shown great energy in gaining control and recruiting soldiers in the eastern provinces. Between them they commanded a huge force of 19 legions and a strong fleet. They also received auxiliary forces from the client kingdoms on Rome's eastern borders. The remaining republicans who had escaped from Italy, such as Cicero's son Marcus Cicero, supported them. Marcus Brutus had visited the philosophical schools in Athens, where he had recruited a number of wealthy young Romans who had been studying there, including the poet Horace (who reached the rank of military tribune despite being the son of a freedman). Cassius had destroyed the Caesarian forces in the east and compelled their leader Publius Cornelius Dolabella, Cicero's son-in-law, to commit suicide. Marcus Brutus had also ordered the execution of Mark Antony's younger brother Gaius, whom he had held in custody for some time after hearing of the death of Cicero and the proscriptions. Antony and Octavian between them now commanded an even larger force of 28 legions—over 100,000 men. This was a similar number of legions to the force that Augustus later used to control the whole empire in peacetime. At the time these were the largest forces that the Romans had ever put in the field. The logistical difficulties of deploying and feeding armies of this size must have been immense and presented great challenges to the organisational ability of all these leaders.

Not even the best of Octavian's presentation skills could ever turn the Philippi campaign into a personal triumph. All the evidence suggests that Octavian's retrospective 'spin' was heavily defensive. In fact, the Caesarian victory represented the high point of Mark Antony's prestige and power in the Roman world. The Mutina campaign was a narrow escape for Antony, and his natural position as Julius Caesar's logical successor had been threatened. Aulus Hirtius had outwitted him at the two battles of Mutina, and only Hirtius' death had prevented his humiliation. Prestige and reputation were just as important as the actual result in a Roman battle, and both Julius Caesar and now Octavian had demonstrated what could be achieved by political propaganda.

The strategic situation was very similar to the one that had faced Caesar when he confronted Pompey. Antony and Octavian were faced by the resources of the Greek east and by a more powerful republican navy. Unlike Caesar, Antony and Octavian possessed a clear advantage in manpower. Just as Caesar had done, they managed to embark their large force in western Greece before being engaged by the main republican navy. Octavian suffered from illness from the start of the campaign, but he was determined to be present at the battle so that Antony would not acquire all the prestige as victor. Brutus and Cassius gathered their forces in Macedonia, and the site for the decisive battle at Philippi was not far from Pharsalus in Thessaly, where Caesar had defeated Pompey.

There were in fact two battles of Philippi. At the first, on 23 October 42 BC, Antony's forces on the right wing routed Cassius' men on the republican left. This should have been decisive, as Cassius was a much more experienced commander than Marcus Brutus. However the republicans had strengthened Brutus' legions on their own right wing, and Marcus Brutus forced

Octavian's troops to retreat. Octavian had to evacuate his own command tent and only narrowly evaded capture. Even Velleius Paterculus, who used Augustus' autobiography as his main source for his account of the battles at Phillipi, admits that Octavian had to flee and records the story that he had been warned by his doctor to escape (Velleius Paterculus, *History of Rome*, 2.70.1). Cassius had been confused about the outcome of the battle after Antony had raided his camp, and he committed suicide to avoid capture. Losses on both sides had been huge. The result of this first battle was certainly indecisive, and Marcus Brutus remained in control of a powerful army.

The second battle of Philippi took place three weeks later. Each side had attempted to regroup and to outmanoeuvre the other. The commanders must have been frantically training their men and preparing for the decisive encounter. The Caesarians were cut off from their supplies, and so Marcus Brutus considered trying to avoid battle. However, the death of Cassius had damaged morale among his troops and some of the non-Roman auxiliaries forces began to desert. Brutus therefore decided to allow a second pitch battle. Once again it was a bloody encounter between two evenly matched armies, but Antony's forces again made the decisive breakthrough leading to victory. When he saw that defeat was inevitable, Marcus Brutus followed Cassius' example and committed suicide.

After the battle of Philippi, Mark Antony was regarded as the leading man in the empire. Octavian gained little prestige, but at least he had survived and the cause of vengeance for Julius Caesar had prevailed. The triumvirate had proved its worth in battle. Octavian had established himself as the second most powerful man in the empire. Lepidus' absence from the battle of Philippi reflects his subordinate role, and Octavian continued to drive him to the margins of effective power.

CHAPTER 4

THE BATTLE FOR THE EMPIRE
42–30 BC

After his decisive role in the victory at Philippi, Antony was in a powerful position when the triumvirs came to negotiate responsibilities. Antony and Octavian both agreed to diminish the influence of Lepidus, who had much less prestige amongst the soldiers. They divided up control of the western provinces between themselves. Antony retained control of Gaul, except the Cisalpine province, which was added to Italy. Octavian received Spain and Sardinia. Lepidus kept control only of Africa, and was now little more than a provincial governor. Octavian was also allocated two difficult tasks. He was required to defeat Sextus Pompeius, who had survived Julius Caesar's victories in Spain and built up a powerful naval force manned by freed slaves. Some of the surviving republicans put themselves under his protection. He was also required to settle the veterans from the Philippi campaign onto farmland in Italy. Perhaps Antony hoped that these two challenges might be beyond his younger rival; he could have been under no illusions about Octavian's ambitions after his actions leading up to the Mutina campaign; he may have been confident, though, that his greater power, wealth and influence would restrain the young Caesar.

Antony showed no desire to suppress his colleagues in his period of supremacy, but he was happy to take on the most prestigious responsibility of settling the eastern half of the empire. The eastern provinces were much the wealthiest and contained many large and prosperous cities. Ephesus and Pergamum in Asia and Antioch in Syria were three of the largest and richest. Antony needed to organise the client kingdoms on Rome's frontiers and to safeguard Syria against invasion by the Parthians. Once he had achieved this, he decided to pursue Caesar's plan to avenge Crassus and invade the Parthian Empire. It was the failure of this expedition that gave Octavian the opportunity to launch a military attack on his colleague.

Octavian's first challenge was to organise the settlement of the soldiers who had survived Philippi. The triumvirs took on the responsibility to settle the surviving troops of the defeated army. One estimate is that Octavian had to find land for 100,000 men. The triumvirs' policy was that veterans must be settled in Italy, but there was simply not enough vacant land available. Thus Octavian had to confiscate land from any community that had harboured sympathy for his opponents or who were simply not strong enough to defend their interests. Land was taken from at least 18 Italian towns. Virgil's *Eclogues* reflect the desperate atmosphere of the period. Virgil himself expresses his gratitude that he was allowed to keep his inherited estates near Mantua, but he also poignantly expresses sympathy for those who lost their land (*Eclogues*, I). The level of social and economic upheaval must have been staggering, and Octavian required all his political capital to enforce this brutal policy.

These confiscations made Octavian very unpopular with the evicted farmers. However, in the long term this programme became the foundation for his military and political strength. By creating settlements of veterans, he gained a large number of clients in Italy who would become his central power base for the future. This clientele became a rich source for military recruitment for the great confrontations that he would face.

Bearing in mind the political shrewdness that he showed in the rest of his career, Octavian may well have made this calculation when he agreed to enact this unpopular policy. Antony certainly failed to realise the ultimate cost of passing this responsibility on to his rival.

The short-term consequences of the redistribution of land created immediate dangers for Octavian. By 41 BC the inhabitants of Etruria and Umbria, where the confiscations were particularly harsh, were prepared for military action. The triumvirs had agreed the appointments of the governing magistrates in Rome, and one of the consuls for 41 BC was Lucius Antonius, Mark Antony's brother. Lucius Antonius organised the opponents of Octavian into a substantial military force of eight legions and resisted further land confiscation. A majority of the senators in Italy supported him, as did Mark Antony's wife, Fulvia, who had not accompanied her husband to the east. There has been a great deal of speculation as to what extent Lucius Antonius communicated with his elder brother about his support for the dispossessed farmers. The likelihood is that he acted on his own initiative. Mark Antony had agreed that the veterans of Philippi must be settled, and it was in his interests for this to happen with as little trouble as possible. Furthermore, the actions of Antony's supporters do not show evidence of any consistent strategy. In contrast, Octavian's response was decisive and typically ruthless.

Octavian ordered Salvidienus, one of his leading supporters, to bring back six legions who were marching to Spain. Marcus Agrippa was already with him to draw up military plans. The provincial governors in Gaul such as Pollio and Plancus, who were loyal to Mark Antony, monitored Octavian's troop movements, but they did not attack his forces or march in support of Lucius Antonius. Thus Octavian was able to bring up an overwhelming force, and compelled Lucius Antonius to withdraw to the town of Perusia. After being besieged, Lucius Antonius surrendered in the early months of 40 BC. Octavian spared him and dispatched him to be governor of Spain, where he died not long afterwards. Fulvia also died shortly after being reunited with Mark Antony in Athens. Octavian showed little mercy either to the citizens of Perusia or to senators who had taken refuge in the town. He handed over the town to be sacked by his ravenous troops, and executed large numbers of his opponents. The fate of Perusia caused terror in Italy and daunted any potential opponents of Octavian. Propertius, the poet, was one of few who were brave enough to lament the victims (Propertius, *Elegies*, I.22.3–4).

Communication across the empire took a considerable time, and Mark Antony was probably only fully informed about events when Octavian had already taken Perusia. His response was to return to Italy in person with a large fleet and a powerful military force, and to besiege the strategic town of Brundisium in the south of Italy. This action was merely an assertive start to negotiations, rather than a determined attempt to destroy Octavian. Antony made contact with his own old enemy, Sextus Pompeius, to strengthen his position; tactical considerations rather than ideology or past history were now becoming the most important factors behind the strategies of the contending leaders in this period. Octavian was certainly not strong enough to confront the forces of Antony, Lepidus and Sextus Pompeius together, and he must have been anxious to prevent his rivals combining against him. Octavian also entered into negotiations with Pompeius and married Scribonia, the daughter of Pompeius' close ally Lucius Scribonius Libo. This marriage only lasted for a short time, but Scribonia was the mother of Octavian's only child, Julia. Octavian found her bad temper intolerable and divorced her the day after Julia's birth.

Julia was taken from her mother and brought up in Octavian's household.

Octavian's precarious position was greatly helped by the fact that the Caesarian legions were reluctant to fight each other at this time. Octavian had endured unpopularity when he secured the interests of Caesarian soldiers and, although the dispossessed inhabitants of Italy hated him, he was still popular among the legionaries. In the engagements at Brundisium, his agents were successful in diminishing the will of Antony's men to fight. Thus Antony, rather than risk mutiny, agreed to meet Octavian and renegotiate the settlement between them.

The treaty they concluded was known as the pact of Brundisium. Octavian's chief negotiator was Gaius Cilnius Maecenas, who became one of Octavian's two most important assistants. The other assistant was Agrippa, whose help was crucial because of his military skill. Octavian had the good sense to realise that his friend was a much more effective general than he was himself, and delegated the responsibility of tactical command to him. Maecenas was famed for his skill in political advice and diplomacy. From this period, the former advisers of Julius Caesar such as Balbus and Oppius became less prominent, and Octavian relied more on his closest friends. Maecenas is most famous to posterity as the sponsor of the great Augustan poets, including Propertius, Virgil, Horace and Ovid. His generous sponsorship encouraged these writers to compose powerful poems to praise Augustus' achievements and to ensure the power of his political legacy. We know that Maecenas travelled to Brundisium in the company of the poets Horace and Virgil on the way to later negotiations with Antony in 37 BC, preparing for the treaty of Tarentum. Horace wrote a fascinating poem (*Satires*, I. 5. 31f) that focuses on the delights of the journey with his friends. He only alludes briefly to the political significance of the journey, but the historical circumstances make the poem seem much more serious.

Maecenas' work at Brundisium in 40 BC was certainly of great value to Octavian, as he survived the crisis with his power intact. Antony and Octavian agreed that Lepidus should control Africa. Octavian would control all the western provinces, and Antony would have a completely free hand in the east. Both leaders would have the right to recruit soldiers in Italy. Fulvia had conveniently died in Greece, and thus a critical component of the treaty was that Antony would marry Octavian's beautiful and virtuous sister, Octavia. Antony must have hoped that this marital alliance would create a permanent bond with his ambitious brother-in-law, but it would prove no more effective in creating a permanent peace than Pompey's marriage to Julius Caesar's daughter.

As relations between Antony and Octavian grew warmer for a short time, Antony revealed to Octavian that Salvidienus, one of Octavian's closest confidants, had been in secret negotiations with his enemies. Octavian quickly arranged for Salvidienus to be captured and executed. This is one of the rare examples of Octavian being deserted by a political associate, but his response was typically decisive and cold-blooded. His supporters learnt that the rewards for loyalty were high, but the price of betrayal would be death.

Once the immediate threat from Antony was allayed, Octavian took action to make a short-term settlement with Sextus Pompeius. He was not yet strong enough to attack Sextus Pompeius in his island strongholds; Sextus Pompeius called himself the son of Neptune because of the strength of his naval forces, and was able to conduct regular raids along the coasts of Italy and to blockade grain supplies from the eastern provinces. In 39 BC Octavian agreed the treaty of Misenum with Pompeius, which conceded to him control over Sardinia, Corsica, Sicily and the Peloponnese (southern Greece). Sextus Pompeius was also promised the consulship for 35 BC. This treaty made Pompeius briefly the third most powerful man in the empire. Augustus later used all his black arts of propaganda to insult Pompeius and to reduce his importance in the histories. However, he was certainly an important and interesting figure in these years.

A significant result of Octavian's treaty with Pompeius was that a number of his supporters who had survived the proscriptions and the civil wars were allowed to return to Rome. One of these men was Tiberius Claudius Nero, descendant of one of the oldest patrician families in Rome, who returned with his beautiful young wife Livia Drusilla and his infant son Tiberius. Livia also belonged to a branch of the Claudian family and was well connected to the republican aristocracy.

Octavian seems to have swiftly fallen in love with Livia. Already his political position was sufficiently strong that traditional social conventions were no barrier to his wishes. Although Livia was pregnant with Tiberius Claudius Nero's child, Octavian arranged for a swift divorce and then married her on 17 January 38 BC. Her son Drusus was born three months after the wedding. Tiberius Claudius Nero died five years later and Octavian adopted his sons. They both became successful generals under Augustus' auspices and 52 years later the son Tiberius succeeded Augustus as *princeps*, ruler of the empire. Octavian's marriage with Livia brought him useful social prestige and helped him to consolidate his relationship with the surviving families of the Roman elite. All the historical sources describe Livia as politically astute, and she became an important adviser for her husband as he sought to develop his control over Italy.

In the *Res Gestae* (an inscription recording his achievements that Augustus published at the end of his reign and which is one of the most important sources for this period), Augustus did not mention Sextus Pompeius by name, but referred to the long and difficult campaign against him as a victory over pirates (*Res Gestae*, 25). Pompeius did adopt some of the techniques of the Cilician pirates whom his father had defeated, and gained much of his manpower from freedmen and escaped slaves. He certainly proved himself a resourceful and innovative commander. Octavian showed no scruples in rapidly breaking his agreement with him within a year of it being concluded. In 38 BC, after secret negotiations, one of Pompeius' freedmen commanders promised to hand over Sardinia. Octavian must have considered this opportunity too good to miss, and he sent a fleet to take over his new possession. Believing that the momentum of the campaign was in his favour, he then attacked Sicily. Pompeius launched a surprise counter-attack and inflicted heavy losses on Octavian's fleet. Octavian then suffered further casualties when a storm struck his retreating ships.

Octavian's reputation was wounded, but he was not destroyed. After this humiliating defeat—the first in his career so far—he showed the resilience that was so crucial for his success. He appealed for help from Antony at the conference of Tarentum in southern Italy in 37 BC, again using Maecenas as his chief negotiator. Octavian and Antony renewed the powers of the triumvirate for another five years, and Antony agreed to give Octavian 120 ships to use against Sextus Pompeius in return for the promise of 20,000 troops to fight against the Parthians. Antony fulfilled his share of the bargain immediately, but—as we shall see—only 2,000 troops ever arrived in the east in return.

Octavian's next task was to secure vengeance against Sextus Pompeius. Once again, he launched a propaganda campaign to represent Pompeius as a pirate and a threat to the prosperity and security of Italy; he presented himself as the defender of the Italian homeland. He gave Agrippa the task of building up the fleet and training the sailors. Agrippa pursued this task with his usual energy and efficiency: he recruited large numbers of freedmen and conscripted slaves to row his galleys. With Antony's additional ships, Agrippa was ready to launch his fleet in the summer of 36 BC, and he defeated Sextus Pompeius at two successive battles at Mylai and Naulochos. Pompeius then fled in despair to the east. Even after such reverses, Sextus Pompeius was able to raise an army of 10,000 men in the province of Asia, appealing to his father's great name, and he tried to avoid Antony's generals in that province. However, his supporters finally drifted away. Eventually Titius, the nephew of Plancus—the wiliest survivor of the late republic—captured Sextus Pompeius. Titius executed him publicly in the city of Miletus and thus finally wiped out the male line of the family of Pompey the Great.

After Pompeius' flight from Sicily, Octavian came into conflict with Lepidus, who still possessed prestige and authority as triumvir. Lepidus had brought a large force from Africa, and many of Pompeius' men decide to surrender to him. In consequence, his forces in Sicily greatly outnumbered Octavian's. Lepidus decided to challenge Octavian's authority and ordered him to leave Sicily. Octavian used his skills of persuasion and appealed directly to Lepidus' men. Again his agents of subversion (probably centurions who had fought with him or with Julius Caesar) had been hard at work in Lepidus' ranks, and Octavian's skills of persuasion were fortified by his tendency to offer more money than his opponents. The magic of Caesar's name worked its accustomed charm. Lepidus' men deserted in droves and he was humiliated. He surrendered himself to Octavian's mercy. Lepidus had been elected as *pontifex maximus* after the death of Julius Caesar and, for all his ruthlessness, Octavian respected the traditional Roman religion. Thus Lepidus had to surrender his position as triumvir, but he was allowed to live under house arrest at Cape Circei in Campania for 24 years until his death in 12 BC, whereupon Augustus took on the title of *pontifex maximus* himself. Octavian was now in control of almost 40 legions, and he was again faced with the problem of finding land for the veterans. He now decided that he would have to settle his men in the provinces, and this new policy meant that land settlements were not quite so traumatic as they had been after Philippi.

Octavian was also faced with the challenge of what to do with Pompeius' escaped slaves. He returned over 30,000 to those who claimed to be their former owners. This dramatically improved his popularity with the ordinary citizens of Rome. He also crucified around 6,000 whom no one claimed. This brutality against escaped slaves recalled Crassus' harsh punishment of the captives from the defeat of Spartacus' rebellion in 71 BC. Octavian claimed that he had restored safety to Italy. With this greater security economic conditions at last began to improve, and most Italians welcomed this. Octavian's official account of the war was that he had defeated dangerous pirates who had terrorised honest Romans and he later repeated this claim in the *Res Gestae* (*Res Gestae*, 25). Thus he proclaimed a triumph for himself in the tradition of republican generals who had conquered barbarian enemies.

There is no evidence that Antony was disconcerted by Octavian's defeat of Sextus Pompeius. His priority was his own campaign against the Parthians. With hindsight, Antony's political strategy was misguided. Octavian's ambition was such that he would never be content to accept the second place in the empire. Antony could have used men such as Lepidus and Sextus Pompeius as allies against his most dangerous rival. Instead, Octavian was able to overcome his rivals one by one and, after the defeats of Sextus Pompeius and Lepidus, he gradually built up his power so that he was in a position to defeat Antony.

While Octavian was engaged with Sextus Pompeius, Antony's attention was devoted to his long-planned campaign against the Parthians. Now the fabled Cleopatra, Queen of Egypt, enters centre stage in our story. She had seduced Julius Caesar during his stay in Egypt after Pompey the Great's murder in 48 BC, and had given birth to his son, whom she called Caesarion. However, since his mother was not a Roman citizen, Caesarion was not mentioned in Caesar's will and was unlikely to be accepted as Caesar's heir by the Roman legions. Cleopatra had briefly lived in Rome at Caesar's villa on the far side of the Tiber until his assassination. Antony and Cleopatra had first become lovers when she had met him in Tarsus in Cilicia. Antony had travelled back with her to Egypt for the winter of 41/40 BC while Octavian was besieging Lucius Antonius in Perusia. Cleopatra gave birth to Antony's twins, but he left her in the spring and did not see her again for another four years.

After the treaty of Brundisium in 37 BC and Antony's marriage to Octavia, Antony's private life became unusually relevant to public affairs. At first, Antony acted the part of the model Roman husband, and Antony and Octavia had two daughters, who both became the grandmothers of emperors (Caligula and Nero). Antony and his subordinates had successfully halted Parthian attempts to invade Syria. The most important victories were won by the general Publius Ventidius Bassus, who had marched as a prisoner in a Roman triumph as a child and who had risen to wealth and power because of his expertise in managing Julius Caesar's logistics. When granted the responsibilities of command, he proved a highly effective general. He defeated the Parthians in three great battles and returned to Rome as the only Roman general to celebrate a triumph for victories over the Parthians until the Emperor Trajan. Ventidius is the ultimate example of the social mobility that was possible in this age of social revolution.

After his return to the eastern provinces in 37 BC, Antony began to plan for a major invasion of the Parthian Empire. The east beckoned to many Roman generals who wished to rival Alexander: Pompey had won his reputation there; Crassus had lost his standards, his soldiers and his life; Julius Caesar had been planning a great campaign against the Parthians before his assassination. Antony's first setback was that Octavian failed to fulfil his part of the bargain agreed at Tarentum. This must have been especially galling for Antony, as he had scrupulously stuck to his side of the agreement by providing Octavian with many of the ships that he had used to defeat Sextus Pompeius. Antony now sent the pregnant Octavia back to Italy and renewed his affair with Cleopatra. Octavian clearly complained on his sister's behalf, and later used this complaint as a crucial part of his aggressive propaganda against Antony. There is evidence to suggest that Octavian was not as virtuous as he represented himself, even after his marriage with Livia. Suetonius records a wonderfully frank letter of Antony's, which even he describes as 'racy'. Suetonius treats the letter as accurate, and not motivated by malice:

> What has changed you so much? Because I have sex with the queen? She is my wife! Didn't I begin this relationship nine years ago? Do you only sleep with Livia Drusilla? My best wishes, if when you read this letter, you haven't been fooling around with Tertulla or Terentilla or Rufilla or Salvia Titisenia or all of them. Does it matter who you or I get off with? (Suetonius, *The Twelve Caesars*, Augustus, 69)

Antony's Latin is rather more vulgar than my translation, and if this letter is genuine, as Suetonius believed, it is a fascinating fragment of the written style of the blunt soldier.

Aside from any romantic pleasure, Antony's relationship with Cleopatra was vital for his planned campaign. Without the legionaries he had expected from Octavian, he needed more money and more troops, and Cleopatra could provide them even if her soldiers were not of the same quality as the Romans. Before Antony departed for his attack on the Parthians, he formally acknowledged Cleopatra's children as his own and gave them stirring names: Alexander Helios (the sun) and Cleopatra Selene (the moon), thus comparing them to the Greek deities Apollo and Artemis. By spring 36 BC Cleopatra was expecting another child, whom she named Ptolemy Philadelphus. Antony sent her back to Egypt before he crossed the Roman frontier and invaded Parthian territory.

Antony attempted to learn from Crassus' disaster and did not march through the arid plains of Mesopotamia where the Parthian horse archers had proved so deadly. Rather he led his force through the client kingdom of Armenia in the north. He met up with Publius Canidius Crassus, who was commanding his advanced guard, in Armenia. His army by this stage was around 60,000 men, the strongest force in the Roman world; many of the centurions would have been veterans of Philippi. Alongside 16 legions of infantry, he had 10,000 Gallic and Spanish cavalry, and levies from his eastern allies.

With this force Antony successfully marched 500 miles to reach Phraaspa, the capital city of Media, but he was not able to secure his lines of communication. The Parthians were successful in bribing Artavasdes, the Armenian king whom Antony considered an ally. They then attacked and wiped out two of Antony's support legions under Oppius Statianus. Even more significantly, they destroyed much of his artillery and supplies. Thus Antony was unable to storm Phraaspa as planned. He was compelled to lead a difficult retreat, constantly harried by enemy cavalry and short of supplies. He showed his ability as a leader of men and his troops showed their endurance by escaping from their precarious situation despite heavy casualties; one estimate is that they lost one-quarter of their number. However, the blow to Antony's reputation and to his political strength was significant. The victor of Philippi lost his aura of invincibility and he had lost many of his best men in distant lands. The contrast with Octavian's success against Sextus Pompeius was marked. Antony would never appear so formidable again.

Antony must have been furious with Octavian on his return in 35 BC. His first priority, though, was to punish the treachery of King Artavasdes of Armenia. Antony renewed his request for 20,000 troops from Octavian. Now that Sextus Pompeius was beaten and had escaped to the east, Octavian had no justification for not sending them, but Octavian appears to have begun his attempts to undermine Antony from this moment. If he did intend to destabilise his partner, his next move was a masterstroke. Octavian finally released a mere 2,000 troops and sent Octavia to lead them. He claimed this was the best he could manage. Antony was left with a dilemma; if he accepted the troops he would seem to condone Octavian's breach of the treaty of Tarentum. If he refused them he would humiliate his wife Octavia and risk disturbing Roman public opinion. He decided to keep the troops, but sent Octavia away to Athens. It was a very public sign of his breach with her brother, and Octavian represented it as a rebuff to his best efforts and those of Italy. Antony then returned to Cleopatra, both for personal consolation, and because he needed financial help from her once more. They acted as if they were joint consorts of a vast eastern kingdom.

Antony resolved on an aggressive response after his losses in the Parthian campaign, and over the next two years he went some way to restoring his lost *dignitas*. Using the money and men from Cleopatra, he marched into Armenia and put Artavasdes into custody. He proclaimed Armenia a Roman province and placed it under the authority of the faithful Canidius. Crassus had not been avenged, but the eastern flank was now secure, so Antony could concentrate on the threat from Octavian in the west.

Antony's next concern was the presentation of these campaigns. In order to preserve his reputation, it was crucial that he put as positive a 'spin' as possible on these events. In truth his achievements were disappointing given the resources that had been committed. However, he was still the ruler of the Greek-speaking eastern part of Roman territory, and it was important for him to display his wealth and power. Thus Antony decided to hold a triumphal procession in Alexandria. Such ritual was entirely traditional for Roman generals in the Hellenistic east; both Pompey and Caesar had staged similar events. The great celebration became known as the Donations of Alexandria. Antony and Cleopatra were seated on high golden thrones. Cleopatra and Julius Caesar's son, Caesarion, were declared joint monarchs of Egypt. Antony marked the occasion by giving them control of Cyprus, which had been an ancestral possession of the Ptolemies. The children of Antony and Cleopatra were declared monarchs of Rome's eastern possessions. He declared Alexander Helios King of Armenia, Ptolemy Philadelphus King of Syria and Cleopatra Selene as Queen of Libya. This spectacle was clearly designed to give the impression of restoring the Egyptian empire to its greatest extent, but for Rome to be the effective military power in the person of Antony.

The ceremony produced the desired effect in the east, where both provincials and the surrounding kingdoms acknowledged the supremacy of Antony. However, Antony underestimated how Octavian could use the symbolism behind this ceremony to his own advantage. Initially he was subdued in his criticism, which he kept private and confined to his own closest supporters. The triumvirs had agreed, though, that Octavian would be consul in 33 BC, and this gave him the ideal position to undermine Antony's influence in Italy and in the western provinces. Octavian and his faction represented Antony as a renegade Roman, enslaved with desire to a foreign queen. Virgil's *Aeneid* (particularly Book VIII) provides plenty of clues for the slogans and 'sound bites' that Octavian and his supporters would have used. Antony was giving away vast territories that had been won by the honest efforts of Rome's armies. Worse than this, he intended to raise huge armies and to overcome the forces of Italy. He and Cleopatra intended Alexandria to be the capital of their new empire, in which Romans would be slaves to the Egyptians. There was no evidence for any of these allegations, yet Octavian succeeded in stirring up fear in the population of Italy and represented himself as the defender of the traditions of Rome. Not everyone was convinced, but Octavian's propaganda was successful enough for him to command a majority of support in all classes of Italy, and this enabled him both to declare war against Antony and Cleopatra, and to put together a military force that could defeat them.

On 1 January 33 BC Octavian took up his position as consul, and began his term of office by launching a bitter attack on Antony, in particular on his settlement of the eastern provinces. When Antony heard of this, he marched from Armenia to Ephesus, where he set up his capital. He summoned Cleopatra and began to muster his forces, calling for auxiliaries from the eastern kingdoms. He publicly acknowledged Caesarion as the true son and rightful heir of Julius Caesar. This presented a great

threat to Octavian, who had used his position as the adopted
son of Caesar to such great effect. However, this did not help
Antony to diminish Octavian's popularity in Italy. As Cleopatra's
son, Caesarion was regarded as more Egyptian than Roman, so
Octavian's agents could use this announcement to emphasise
the threat from Egypt.

In the beginning of the next year the crisis intensified. The
two consuls for 32 BC, Gaius Sosius and Gnaeus Domitius
Ahenobarbus were both loyal supporters of Antony. Antony
must have hoped that they could help him to recover much of the
support in Italy that he had lost the previous year. Sosius went on
the attack by immediately denouncing the actions of Octavian.
There was a brief return to republican freedom of speech with
the factions of the leaders of east and west bitterly denouncing
each other. Octavian realised that he needed to assert his control
in Rome; he entered the Senate with armed troops, declaring
that the security of the state was at stake. The two consuls were
sufficiently intimidated that they fled to join Antony at Ephesus.
Over 300 senators who were supporters of Antony departed
with them. As the overall membership of the Senate was about
1,000 at this stage, this meant that Octavian had the support of
well over half the Senate. The Antonians realised that civil war
was inevitable and that they had no chance of resisting Octavian
in Italy. For the third time within 20 years forces raised from the
western and eastern provinces prepared for battle.

Antony prepared for the conflict by formally divorcing Octavia.
He had been living with Cleopatra as his wife for at least four
years. This gave further ammunition to Octavian's propaganda
campaign. Antony had scorned his sister, recognised by all as a
virtuous Roman *matrona* (wife) in favour of Cleopatra, who had
enslaved his senses. Many of the Roman senators who had joined
Antony that year were distressed at how influential Cleopatra

was in the council of war. It was vital for Antony to project an image as the rightful leader of Rome and to give a clear vision to his Roman supporters of how he could win this struggle and what he would do with his victory. He may well have attempted to do this. Our sources on Antony's actions at this point are heavily influenced by Augustus' propaganda, and even the accounts that do their best to be neutral, are swayed by the fact of Antony's defeat (e.g. Plutarch, *Life of Antony*). At any rate, Antony was not able to keep the support of influential Roman allies.

At this crucial stage Lucius Munatius Plancus and his nephew Marcus Titius deserted Antony's army and joined Octavian. Plancus was one of the great survivors of the period. He had no senatorial ancestors, but was descended from a wealthy family in the town of Tibur, within 20 miles of Rome. He had risen to prominence as a supporter of Julius Caesar and had been rewarded with the governorship of Gallia Comata. The dictator had designated him as consul for 42 BC. Cicero kept in close touch with him throughout his campaign against Antony in 43 BC, and a number of Plancus' letters in reply survive. He pledges his loyalty to the Republic and his friendship to Cicero in elegant Latin prose (*Letters to his Friends*, X.35.2). However, once Cicero's coalition broke down after the fiasco of the Mutina campaign, he first threw in his lot with Lepidus and Pollio, Caesar's other governors in Gaul, and then put his forces at the service of Antony.

Thus Plancus survived to serve as consul in 42 BC, unlike Decimus Brutus, his prospective colleague. His brother Plotius Plancus lacked his ability to pick the winning side, and he was killed in the proscriptions. Lucius Munatius Plancus served with Antony at Philippi and throughout the next decade he was one of the most influential of Antony's supporters. Plancus had tried to represent Mark Antony's interests in the Perusine War, and had travelled with Antony's wife, Fulvia, to meet Antony in Athens. He had then served as proconsul of Asia at the time of the Parthian invasion, defeated by Ventidius. In 35 BC he was serving as proconsul of Syria, safeguarding Antony's supply lines for his campaigns in Armenia and Media. Titius, his nephew, eventually captured and executed Sextus Pompeius. Thus Plancus was probably the most experienced of all of Antony's supporters and had become a powerful figure in his own right. He was prepared to flatter Cleopatra and used his diplomatic skills to develop his power within Antony's faction.

However, in the autumn of 32 BC both Plancus and his nephew Titius secretly left Antony's camp at Ephesus, made their way to Rome and declared themselves as supporters of Octavian. It is impossible to be sure of their motives, but they must have calculated that Octavian was the most likely winner of the struggle that lay ahead. Antony had mustered 30 legions and had assembled a huge fleet, yet Plancus was an experienced commander and he risked his wealth, his social standing and his life on the judgement that Antony would lose. He must have detected inefficiency in Antony's armed forces, and a lack of clear strategy within the high command. Once again his assessment proved to be shrewd. He deserted at just the right point to gain favour with Octavian. He survived to propose the title of Augustus in 27 BC and to serve as censor in 22 BC.

The moral effect of Plancus' defection must have been immense. He was also able to provide Octavian with precious information to allow him to continue his propaganda campaign. Plancus had been such a trusted confidant of Antony that he had witnessed his last will and testament. He knew that the disclosure of its contents would be deeply wounding to Antony's public image, and very beneficial for Octavian. He confirmed that the Vestal Virgins held this document in Rome. On hearing this information,

Octavian risked the charge of sacrilege by seizing the document by force. The details of Antony's will provided him with valuable evidence to support his accusation that Antony had betrayed the Roman people. Allegedly, Antony left instructions that he should be buried with Cleopatra in Alexandria. He also confirmed the Donations of Alexandria by bequeathing the eastern territories to his children by Cleopatra. Octavian proclaimed that he was stealing the property of the Roman people. These revelations were so convenient for Octavian that it is entirely possible that this will was forged, and the whole story of the revelation by Plancus was staged as a convenient charade to make the charges seem more plausible. The will may have been genuine, but if so, Octavian must have carefully edited how its contents were disclosed to the Senate.

Octavian now had sufficient material to justify a declaration of war. He took great care to declare war against Cleopatra. He treated Antony as her subordinate and as a renegade. There was a carefully organised campaign of misrepresentation to divert both elite and public opinion from the true nature of the war. His agents painstakingly arranged a patriotic campaign in which the people of the cities and towns throughout Italy swore a personal oath of allegiance to him as their commander in war. He later celebrated this declaration in his great inscription, the *Res Gestae*, with the following sentence: 'All Italy swore an oath of allegiance to me of its own free will and chose me as leader for the war I won at Actium' (*Res Gestae*, 25).

Thus Octavian declared himself to be the leader of Italy. Octavian's propaganda campaign had worked particularly well with the *equites*. He gained important support from the communities of Italy and raised large numbers of valuable soldiers from the veterans he had settled on the land ten years before. Despite all his efforts, Octavian was desperately short of money to pay and supply his forces, and thus he levied unprecedented levels of taxation, up to 25 per cent of income, which made a huge economic impact on Italy. The Senate obediently stripped Antony of his planned consulship for the next year, and instead Octavian served as consul for 31 BC with the former republican Marcus Valerius Messalla Corvinus as his colleague. He must have been chosen for his noble connections and to emphasise the breadth of Octavian's coalition against Antony and Cleopatra.

Octavian made the sensible decision to entrust the management of the military strategy of the campaign to Marcus Agrippa. Agrippa was the perfect deputy leader: able, efficient and loyal. He did not have the family connections to become a rival to Octavian, but he proved himself to be a man of great capabilities. In order to defeat Sextus Pompeius, he had greatly improved the military effectiveness of Octavian's armed forces. In particular he had mastered the art of naval warfare, and this would be decisive for the campaign against Antony. Maecenas was entrusted with the management of Italy, while the western provinces were handed over to loyal supporters with skeleton forces. Every man possible was committed to the main force to engage in the east. Antony had moved his army from Ephesus to northern Greece, which would be the centre for a decisive battle between the Romans for the third time within 20 years. Octavian and Agrippa succeeded in transferring their troops across the Adriatic Sea. Although he outnumbered them, Antony did not feel strong enough to attack them directly. Agrippa used his naval forces to cut off Antony and Cleopatra's supply route to Egypt. Thus the efficiency of their main force was rapidly reduced on account of their shortage of provisions and equipment. Octavian then deployed his main force to the south, which meant that Antony was further cut off from his supplies.

Antony had been outmanoeuvred and proved unable to engage the enemy effectively. Morale in his camp continued to dwindle, and he suffered from mass desertion. Many of the eastern kings had joined Antony because they feared his superior force; they were among the first to slip away. One crucial defection was that of Gnaeus Domitius Ahenobarbus. His father had been one of Julius Caesar's most passionate opponents and Gnaeus Domitius Ahenobarbus had fought with Marcus Brutus and Cassius at Philippi. Antony had spared him then, and Ahenobarbus had become one of his most important supporters. He had always distrusted Cleopatra's influence, but had remained loyal when Plancus had fled. Despairing of Antony's chances and of what his cause had become, he saved his family's wealth by surrendering to Octavian.

On 2 September 31 BC Antony launched a naval attack. Military analysts now see Antony's plan for the battle as a gamble to break out from a hopeless position, rather than as a serious attempt to defeat Octavian's forces. Thus Virgil's description in *Aeneid*, Book VIII, following the official line, is deeply misleading. Augustus wanted to celebrate a glorious victory; but although military historians may enjoy a victory based on superior planning and deployment, it does not make great propaganda. Thus Augustus' friends and admirers would describe Actium as a brave victory in an epic set-piece battle. The best historical evidence suggests that the truth was rather different. The actual fighting was rather light. Many of Antony's ships surrendered; Cleopatra led the breakout, and Antony was able to follow her, but only a small fraction of his great army escaped with him.

The battle of Actium may not have been as dramatic as Pharsalus or Philippi, but it was just as decisive. Antony's legions on the mainland surrendered after negotiating the terms that their lives would be spared and that they would be honourably discharged with grants of land in the provinces. Again Octavian's agents had been at work to spread disaffection in the rival camp. A desperate engagement with Antony's remaining land forces would have been an unnecessary risk. Instead, Octavian's political skills made sure that this threat was avoided. Now in a position of strength, Octavian went back to Julius Caesar's policy of *clementia*. Most of the opposition commanders were spared.

Octavian did not hurry to pursue Antony and Cleopatra to Egypt. He was determined to wipe them out rather than let them survive as a potential danger to his domination. However, he took care to safeguard his own position first. Antony's prestige had been fatally weakened by the Actium campaign. Octavian could now draw on the full resources of Rome, whereas Antony and Cleopatra only controlled Ptolemaic Egypt. Octavian first returned to Italy to deal with the demands of discontented veterans. Once he had ensured his control over Italy and the western provinces he put together an army to defeat Antony and Cleopatra definitively. Gaius Cornelius Gallus led a force from the Roman province of Africa. Octavian himself led the main army marching south from Syria. There was almost a year between Octavian's victory at Actium and his final assault on Alexandria, but Antony and Cleopatra were not able to marshal any effective resistance to defend their capital.

Antony made one final attempt to attack Octavian's vanguard outside Alexandria, but when his forces were beaten off he committed suicide. Cleopatra remained alive for a few more days. Octavian put her into custody and interviewed her personally. The historical sources then record that Cleopatra committed suicide by smuggling in a poisonous snake to kill both herself and her maids. There are two important difficulties with this traditional account. First, it would have been difficult for Cleopatra to ensure that the snakebite would be fatal. Second, the sources describe the deaths of Cleopatra and her maids as happening very quickly, which is not usually the case with the bites of Egyptian snakes. It is certainly plausible that the story in the historical sources was devised by Octavian to cover up Cleopatra's secret execution. Whatever the truth of this, Octavian ruthlessly killed the other most dangerous captives. Caesarion was executed, despite his youth. Octavian knew that a natural son of Caesar could become a rival. He also ordered the execution of Antony's oldest son, Antyllus.

Thus, 14 years after his first march on Rome, Octavian finally possessed undisputed control over the Roman territories. He was still only 33 years old. He had the same level of power that Julius Caesar had possessed in 45 BC. This precedent was disconcerting, and Octavian now faced the challenge of proving that he had the vision to justify his ambition. Until 27 BC Octavian had proved himself as the toughest competitor in the vicious struggle for power. His great challenge would be to fulfil the hopes of his supporters and to create a lasting settlement.

PART III

Caesar Augustus

CHAPTER 5

THE RES PUBLICA OF AUGUSTUS

After the defeat of Antony and Cleopatra, Octavian had the opportunity to put his vision for the Roman state into practice. His first significant decision was to add Egypt to Rome's territories. He set up a different system of administration there to that of the other provinces. He claimed Egypt as his own personal possession and appointed a prefect of equestrian rank, Cornelius Gallus, to administer it. He forbade senators from entering Egypt, where his authority was much like a king's. Octavian had all the autocratic powers of a pharaoh although he ruled in absence as the Persian kings had done. Most importantly, the wealth that Octavian acquired in Egypt from the treasury of Cleopatra gave him significant financial resources to reward his followers and to carry out his plans.

On his return to Rome Octavian held a triumph for his victories at Actium and at Alexandria. He emphasised his achievement by ordering the gates of Janus to be closed. This rare ceremony indicated that Rome was at peace. Octavian could now claim to have brought security and stability to Italy. A few senators might regret the end of republican liberty in private, but the vast majority of the inhabitants of Italy were greatly relieved that the civil wars appeared to be over, and they were loyal to Octavian as the leader who could preserve civic harmony.

Octavian's first challenge was to organise the retirement of a large number of soldiers. After the Actium campaign he controlled 60 legions of his own and Antony's men. He decided that a force of 28 legions was sufficient to control the territory and that the state could afford to pay these legions as a professional standing army. He settled many of the surviving soldiers on settlements called *coloniae* in Italy and in the provinces. The money he had acquired in Egypt meant that he could achieve this by purchasing land rather than by confiscations. The payment of 60 legions had nearly bankrupted Rome, and he and his successors continued to wrestle with the difficulty of funding the pay and the retirement even of the reduced force of 28 legions.

Once he had completed this task, Octavian was faced with the dilemma of determining his political position. Since the emergencies that had led to the extraordinary power of the triumvirs were over, Octavian needed a new basis to establish his rule. Open authoritarianism had been discredited by the failure of Julius Caesar and Mark Antony, but Octavian was equally unwilling to follow Sulla's example of restoring the power of the Senate and retiring into private life. The bitter divisions of the past century demonstrated that a new system of government was needed, but the assassination of Caesar proved that any solution must be palatable to the senatorial class. Thus Augustus took care to soothe the sensibilities of the Roman nobility. He deliberately used conciliatory language to hide the reality of his own power.

The historian Cassius Dio, writing in the third century AD, composed an instructive fictional debate between Agrippa and Maecenas, which he set in 29 BC. He made Agrippa argue for the return of the republic and for Octavian to give up his authoritarian power (Cassius Dio, *Roman History*, LII.2–41). In reality Agrippa was too much of a realist to have ever argued for this policy, but Octavian and his closest advisers must have

*1 The Pantheon: even though the main construction of the Pantheon
was carried out under Hadrian, the inscription of Agrippa's name
demonstrates his importance*

considered the consequences if he genuinely gave up his power.
The likelihood is that Octavian's retirement would have led to
further civil conflict. In the second half of the debate Maecenas
argues effectively for a monarchy and for a detailed reorganisation
of Rome's government. In the end this was the option that
Octavian chose, but he took great care to avoid giving offence
to those who valued the republican past. Octavian took his time
to bring forward his new system of government. From 31 BC he
served as one of Rome's two consuls, and for the crucial years
of 28 BC and 27 BC the two consuls were Octavian and Agrippa.
In 28 BC Octavian declared that all the emergency powers that
he had taken in the civil wars were now invalid. He then faced

two political crises that must have influenced the details of his political settlement.

Marcus Licinius Crassus, the grandson of Crassus, Julius Caesar's ally in the first triumvirate, was one of the few surviving aristocrats who might potentially challenge Octavian's authority. He had supported Octavian at Actium and was rewarded with the consulship for 30 BC. He then served as a proconsular governor of Macedonia. He commanded legions on the frontier and by defeating the neighbouring tribes he acquire territory for Rome. As a reward for these achievements Crassus requested not only a triumph, but also the unusual honour of the *spolia opima*. This military decoration was granted for killing the enemy

2 *Seated portrait of Tiberius from the Vatican Museums*

leader in single combat and had only been awarded twice in the history of the republic, after Romulus had won it, according to legend. This award would have raised Crassus' public distinction to a dangerous level. Octavian did not deny that Crassus had killed the enemy commander, but decreed that he had to be fighting under his own auspices as a serving consul to earn this prestigious decoration. Crassus was granted a triumph in 27 BC, but was refused the *spolia opima*. He is not mentioned again in the historical record; presumably Augustus ensured that he retired into private life and had no further opportunity to set himself up as a rival to the *princeps'* glory.

Octavian's second crisis concerned Cornelius Gallus, the prefect of Egypt. Gallus was a renowned elegiac poet and a friend of Virgil, who dedicated the tenth *Eclogue* in his honour. He incurred Octavian's displeasure because of his excessive concern to publicise his own achievements. He allowed statues of himself rather than his superior to be erected in many Egyptian towns, and he ordered the Egyptians to carve his own name on the pyramids. An interesting inscription reveals that he boasted that he led his troops further south in Egypt than any previous Roman leader (Dessau, *Inscriptiones Latinae Selectae*, 8995). The Senate condemned him in 28 BC, and Gallus committed suicide in 27 BC. Augustus replaced Cornelius Gallus with Marcus Aelius Gallus, a more pedestrian figure. Augustus clearly regarded the province of Egypt as very significant and considered it vital that the prefect was absolutely loyal and subordinate to him.

Thus when Octavian finally revealed his new settlement he was well aware that he needed to establish his power on a secure legal basis, and that he needed to safeguard his position from potential rivals. Octavian organised this announcement carefully and prepared his supporters to lead the response of the Senate. On 13 January 27 BC Octavian proclaimed that he was returning all his powers and provinces to the Senate and Roman people. The senators immediately protested that the state could not survive without his leadership. Loyal senators requested that Octavian should take the responsibility to administer the most important military provinces, namely Spain, Gaul and Syria, for ten years with proconsular authority. Octavian made a show of reluctance but accepted this proposal. He remained in Rome as consul, and legates administered these provinces on his behalf, and were answerable to his authority. There was a republican precedent for this measure, as the Senate had given a similar command over Spain to Pompey. However, Augustus' command was much bigger and included the overwhelming majority of Rome's military force. The time limit was important, as it appeared that Octavian was a constitutionally appointed leader. Octavian submitted to time limits for a number of his responsibilities. When they had run out, he simply secured a further term. Senior former magistrates from the Senate would govern the less strategic provinces as proconsuls and propraetors.

The next phase of the settlement concerned Octavian's personal position and honours. Lucius Munatius Plancus, the great survivor, proposed that the Senate should grant Octavian the title *Augustus*, which can be translated as 'the illustrious one'. Octavian selected this name carefully. He had rejected the name Romulus as too closely associated with monarchy. The name Augustus carried associations with Rome's traditional religion. Thus Augustus (as I will call him for the rest of the book) now declared his name as *Imperator Caesar divi filius Augustus*. The use of *imperator* as a name stressed his military power and his victories. His declaration that he was son of the deified Caesar would have appealed to the loyalty of his soldiers and to the urban poor in Rome. The name Augustus now signified his dignity and authority. The senators also voted Augustus two particular symbolic honours that he later recorded in the *Res Gestae* (*Res Gestae*, 34). They decreed that they should place a laurel wreath above the doorposts of his house to indicate that he had saved the lives of Roman citizens. They also hung a golden shield in the Senate House, proclaiming Augustus' virtues of clemency, courage, justice and piety. These four virtues would feature prominently in Augustus' subsequent propaganda. They made up a manifesto that was easy to understand and which appealed to the traditional values of Rome and Italy.

Augustus later interpreted this settlement of 27 BC in two well-known passages in the *Res Gestae* (34 and 35). He stated that he possessed no greater power than his fellow magistrates but that he surpassed them in authority. He also proclaimed that he had transferred constitutional government to the Senate and people. The aim of his rhetoric is clear. The source of his power is meant to be constitutional and based on consent. Nevertheless the reality of Augustus' control was obvious. Senators, soldiers, citizens and provincials were all well aware that Augustus was the ruler of Rome. Augustus controlled far greater personal wealth than any other Roman, and he had a much wider range of clients. He could determine the composition of the Senate and control Rome's foreign policy. All these powers were covered in the *Res Gestae* under the deliberately vague term *auctoritas*.

The settlement of 27 BC was merely the first step in Augustus' definition of his position. As subsequent events revealed potential political difficulties, he refined his legislation to fit the circumstances. Augustus took seriously the responsibility of his provincial commands and in 27 BC he departed for Spain, where he presided over military operations to exert Roman control over the north-west corner of the Iberian Peninsula (which the Romans had not yet fully subdued). He continued to possess authority as one of the two consuls, and returned to Rome in 24 BC before the campaign was complete.

Augustus made his first attempt to promote the younger generation of his family in these years. Augustus and Livia did not have any children from their own marriage, although they both had children from their previous spouses. Marcellus, the son of Augustus' sister Octavia, married Augustus' daughter Julia in 25 BC. The next year Marcellus was elected aedile at the age of 18, and was granted the right to stand for the consulship ten years before he reached the minimum age. It appeared that Augustus was grooming Marcellus as his successor to head the ruling family. However, Marcellus' growing prominence led to tension within the Roman government. Marcus Primus, the governor of Macedonia, was charged with making war without permission. In his trial Primus claimed to be acting on the private orders of Augustus and (more plausibly) Marcellus. The senatorial jury rejected Primus' claims after Augustus had denied them in person, and they found Primus guilty, which ended his political career. This affair does seem to have weakened Marcellus position in the imperial household.

In 23 BC Augustus' effective intelligence service uncovered a plot against his life involving a young republican noble, Fannius Caepio. Augustus' soldiers killed Caepio and some other conspirators who apparently resisted arrest. Augustus also accused a certain Varro Murena of supporting this conspiracy, and he was convicted and executed. His disgrace affected the standing of his brother-in-law, Maecenas. Soon after the defeat of this plot, Augustus suffered a serious illness. He clearly feared for his life and entrusted his signet ring to Agrippa and his official papers to his colleague as consul, Calpurnius Piso. Augustus survived the crisis thanks to intervention of his doctor Antonius Musa, but his nephew Marcellus died of an illness in the same year. Virgil moving refers to the death of Marcellus at the end of Book VI of the *Aeneid* (*Aeneid*, VI.863–86). Under Antonius Musa's supervision, Augustus' health dramatically improved and he lived to the age of 75, despite the serious illnesses of his youth.

Augustus' response to these events was to give up the consulship. The fact that he had held down one of the two consulships each year had meant that it was harder for him to reward his supporters with the most important political honour. In place of the consulship, Augustus received two important additions to his power. First he was granted *maius imperium*, meaning 'greater power'. This ensured that he could officially override the orders of any other provincial governor. This additional power strengthened his authority over the provinces. Even more importantly, Augustus received *tribunicia potestas*. The Gracchi had shown how much power the tribunes could wield; now Augustus represented himself as the guardian of the citizens of Rome. His tribunician power meant that he could propose laws before the Senate whenever he wished, and that he had a right of veto and also the ability to grant an amnesty to any citizen accused of a crime. The tribunician power became one of Augustus' most important titles. He referred to it on his coins and on other inscriptions, and used it as the official measure of the length of his rule. The fact that tribunician power was later granted to Agrippa and subsequently to Tiberius marked them out as the second most powerful men in the empire. A vital advantage of this honour was that it carried popular connotations and, as it harked back to the traditions of the republic, it was not especially offensive to the aristocracy. As well as the leader of the Senate, Augustus was now the guardian of the freedom and welfare of the Roman people.

Between 22 BC and 19 BC Augustus was absent from Rome, organising the eastern provinces and conducting successful negotiations with the Parthians to secure the return of the standards lost by Crassus at the battle of Carrhae in 53 BC. In 19 BC there was a significant challenge to Augustus' authority. Egnatius Rufus had been an energetic and popular aedile who had organised conscripted slaves to act as a fire brigade in Rome. He was elected praetor and offered himself as a candidate for the consulship, but was rejected by the consul Gaius Sentius Saturnius, who was governing Rome on Augustus' behalf. Egnatius Rufus led a series of riots to protest against this decision, but he was captured and executed on the charge of plotting against Augustus' life. Augustus returned to Rome soon after Rufus' death. Cassius Dio records that in 19 BC Augustus was granted consular powers for life (*Roman History*, LIV.10). He received the right to exercise consular *imperium* in Rome and Italy; he had the authority to give orders both in Italy and in the provinces. This new power made it easier to suppress civil disorder, and clarified Augustus' power within Italy itself.

Augustus did not need to grant himself any further powers after 19 BC. There is little record of civil disturbance after this period. Augustus had demonstrated his total control over the state. The sensible action for the upper classes was to support his rule. The poorer classes regarded Augustus as their champion. There seems to have been little nostalgia for the republic in this period—the sentiment seems only to have arisen after the shortcomings of Augustus' successors became obvious in the next century. After 19 BC, Roman politics entered a new phase. The constitution remained stable, but the balance of power changed depending on relations within the ruling family. Augustus had now established a secure basis for his own power, and he now pursued a number of different goals, such as expanding the empire, improving social behaviour, securing the succession and projecting his legacy.

CHAPTER 6

THE FRONTIERS OF EMPIRE

O nce Augustus had secured power over the Roman Empire, he intended to use his armed forces to assert Rome's military strength. Augustus' final advice to his successor Tiberius warning against extending the empire is well known, but his own imperial policy was aggressive for most of his rule. *Virtus*, meaning military valour, was one of his four virtues praised by the Senate in 27 BC. Indeed, in the 40 years of Augustus' rule, the Roman Empire gained more territory than at any time in its previous history. It was only the military losses of the last years that made him more cautious. He presided over a significant expansion of the empire's frontiers, and his intentions were even more dramatic.

Even before the battle of Actium, in 35 BC Augustus had led his armies beyond the Roman boundaries of the province of Illyricum (modern Croatia). One purpose of this campaign had been to train his legions to fight against Antony, but he also aimed to secure trade and communication routes between Italy and Greece. Once he had defeated Antony, Augustus' first military campaign was in Spain. He briefly commanded the army himself, but he entrusted the rest of the campaign to his legates, who eventually gained control of the whole peninsula after hard fighting. Agrippa supervised the final stage of this offensive in 19 BC.

Augustus' primary concern after 24 BC was the eastern frontier. His first advance took place after the death of King

Amyntas of Galatia died in 25 BC. Galatia was a client kingdom bordering on Rome's borders in central and eastern Turkey, and contained cities such as Ancyra and Iconium. Augustus took over the kingdom as a province without difficulty. His most important policy for the eastern empire was to secure the border with the Parthian Empire. He rejected Antony's decision to invade Parthian territory. Instead his plan was to achieve his aims by negotiation and intrigue.

For the first ten years after Actium, Augustus welcomed envoys from the Parthian king, and bided his time. However, once he had strengthened his own armies, Augustus took advantage of an opportunity in 20 BC to negotiate from a position of strength. The key to Roman relations with Parthia was control over the strategic kingdom of Armenia. Antony had attempted to hold Armenia as a Roman province, but the Parthians had regained control of the kingdom after the battle of Actium and had set up a client king of their own called Artaxes. In 20 BC the Parthian king Phraates IV was distracted by a dispute with a rival claimant to the throne called Tiridates. Tiridates appealed for Roman help, and Augustus used a network of agents to act in his favour. He also used Rome's influence in Armenia to develop a conspiracy against the Parthian puppet, Artaxes.

Once he had set up the diplomatic circumstances to his own advantage, Augustus mobilised a large army to march to the eastern frontier. His stepson Tiberius was now old enough to play an important role, and he commanded Augustus' vanguard. Augustus himself waited with the main army in reserve in Syria while Tiberius led his forces into Armenia. The Armenian opposition conveniently assassinated Artaxes, and Tiberius crowned Rome's nominee Tigranes as King of Armenia. This action signified that Armenia was now within Rome's sphere of influence. Phraates desperately offered concessions to stave off a full invasion of Parthia. He offered to return the captured standards that had been a painful symbol of the humiliation of Crassus and Antony. He also released Roman prisoners, a few of whom had lived as Parthian slaves for 34 years. Thus Augustus had established peace with security on the most vulnerable frontier of the empire.

When the east was secure, Augustus could move on to his great strategic design on the northern European frontier of the Roman Empire. The first phase of his plan was to ensure the security of northern Italy by controlling the whole of the Alpine range. This objective required Augustus to create new provinces in Raetia and Noricum (modern Switzerland and Austria). This would take the frontier up to the Danube River. The second segment of his plan was to advance up to the Danube north from Illyricum, Macedonia and Thrace; this would thus create two further provinces of Pannonia and Moesia. The third and most difficult phase was to conquer Germany up to the Elbe River. This would shorten communications between the Rhine and the Danube and would avoid creating a vulnerable frontier north of Ractia and west of the provinces of Germania Superior and Belgica. As we will see, Augustus successfully carried out the first two phases of this plan, and only failed in the third after initial successes.

Augustus himself was based in Gaul from 16 BC to 13 BC. Agrippa looked after the eastern empire and maintained order and stability there with *tribunicia potestas*. The first offensive for Augustus' grand design in the north began in 16 BC. Augustus' two stepsons, Tiberius and Drusus led the main attack from north-eastern Italy; they added Noricum to the empire and reached the Danube. They then moved west to gain control of Raetia. In these campaigns Tiberius began to build the reputation that would establish him as one of Rome's great generals. Although his campaigns are less well known than those of Julius

Caesar or even Agrippa, he was consistently successful at achieving difficult objectives with a low level of Roman casualties. Thus by 14 BC the Romans had created the provinces of Raetia and Noricum as planned and for the first time in the history of the empire, Italy was protected from invasion by unconquered tribes on its borders. These victories were understandably popular in Italy, and Horace celebrated the success of the two young Claudians, Tiberius and Drusus, in his fourth book of *Odes* (Horace, *Odes*, IV.4 and IV.14). The Senate erected a monument known as the Tropaeum Alpium to commemorate the victories under Augustus' authority, and it still survives as a ruin at La Turbie near Monaco.

The second stage of the operation began in 13 BC when Agrippa and Tiberius invaded Pannonia (western Hungary) and Drusus advanced into western Germany. Agrippa's death in 12 BC meant that Tiberius and Drusus were now Augustus' most important deputies. Tiberius took over command of this campaign and spent four years overcoming the tribes of northern Illyria and Pannonia. Again his campaign was successful, and by 8 BC Tiberius had established the new tribute-paying province of Pannonia. The expansion of the empire into Illyria and Pannonia was an important achievement for Augustus as it secured the land route from Italy to Greece, and produced a safe frontier for the entire Mediterranean coast.

Drusus' campaigns in Germany were equally successful. Augustus' legates had maintained stability on the Rhine frontier. Drusus had the time to establish an overwhelming force and to launch a major invasion into the territory of the German tribes. Archaeologists have found a large Roman camp from this era on the river Lippe at Oberaden and a complex supply fort at Beckinghausen, both of which seem to have been designed to enable the legions to spend the winter in Germany. This was a crucial part of preparing a new province. Drusus reached the river Elbe by 9 BC and Augustus must have had great hopes that his campaigns would have the effect of creating a new province of Germania.

The first blow to Augustus' grand design was that Drusus fell from his horse while returning from the Elbe and suffered fatal injuries. His death deprived Augustus of a popular and efficient member of his family. However, Tiberius took over the campaign and conducted it effectively. The historian Velleius Paterculus, who served under Tiberius at this time and who wrote his history of these wars in tribute to his former commander states that by 6 BC Tiberius had subdued Germany up to the Elbe (Velleius Paterculus, *History of Rome*, II.97). Tiberius certainly regarded the situation as safe enough for him to return to Rome. He then shocked Augustus by announcing his wish to retire into private life and to retreat to Rhodes. This decision deprived Augustus of his best commander and most capable deputy.

After Tiberius' retirement, Augustus did not see the need to begin any further aggressive actions in the west. He now set his commanders the difficult task of defeating insurgents and pacifying the inhabitants. At first this seems to have gone well. Although the ruling family was weak during Tiberius' years in Rhodes, Augustus entrusted significant commands to his political supporters. Later historians such as Suetonius and Velleius Paterculus were interested in Tiberius, and so the historical record is less detailed for his years of exile on Rhodes. However, we know that Lucius Domitius Ahenobarbus, who was married to Antony and Octavia's daughter Antonia and the grandfather of the Emperor Nero, led an army from the Danube to the Elbe in this period and that he built a causeway on the far side of the Rhine.

Augustus used another major campaign to promote an intended successor in AD 1. He judged that his grandson Gaius (the son of Agrippa and Julia) was now old enough to lead an army to the east to conduct negotiations and settle the kingdom of Armenia, just as Tiberius had done 12 years before. Initially, Gaius and his advisers carried out Augustus' instructions well. Gaius led an army to the province of Syria and met the Parthian King Phraates V on the Euphrates River. Gaius confirmed the previous agreement that the Romans would continue to control Armenia. However, there was resistance to this agreement from within Armenia itself, and Gaius led his army into Armenia to enforce it. His military campaign was successful, but in AD 3 the young prince was seriously wounded. Gaius died in AD 4 as he attempted to return to Rome. His younger brother Lucius had also died in AD 2, and so Augustus had to look for a new successor. Since he regarded Agrippa Postumus, the third son of Agrippa and Julia, as unsuitable, and Drusus' son Germanicus was too young, he had little choice but to bring back Tiberius to military command.

Once Tiberius was back in favour, he again took up command of the armies in Germany. In AD 4 he led both a fleet and an army to the Elbe; the following year he was preparing a large expedition to attack King Marbod and his Marcomanni tribe in the modern day Czech Republic. The aim of this expedition was to provide a link from Drusus' conquests in northern Germany to the new provinces of Pannonia and Noricum. Tiberius had actually set out for this campaign with 12 legions when he heard of a dangerous revolt in the new province of Pannonia. Thus Tiberius was compelled to abandon the planned attack, and to come to the defence of Pannonia. The ageing Augustus was clearly concerned by the threat from the united Pannonian tribes, and he organised the conscriptions of both slaves and citizens to ensure the defence of Italy. Tiberius' forces were strong enough to suppress the revolt by AD 9, but it had required hard fighting.

The strain of continual campaigns was also beginning to tell on Rome's treasury, and Rome was short of money in these years.

However, just as Tiberius' victory in Pannonia was complete and the Roman state had granted him a triumph, Augustus learnt of the worst military disaster of his career. Towards the end of AD 9 Publius Quinctilius Varus, a former consul and trusted legate of Augustus, was in command of three legions. He appears to have been acting as the governor of the province of Germania and had been organising the collection of taxation. Arminius, tribal chief of the Cherusci, had previously been an ally of the Romans and had won Varus' trust. He had studied Roman military methods and was aware of their weaknesses. He treacherously organised an ambush of Varus' three legions as they returned to their winter quarters through the Teutoburgian forest. Arminius achieved total surprise and the Roman legionaries were forced to defend themselves desperately in unfavourable conditions. Arminius succeeded in destroying all three legions, and Varus committed suicide. Arminius ordered that any Roman that tried to surrender should be slaughtered. The battle in the Teutoburgian forest was the greatest Roman defeat since Crassus' disaster at Carrhae 62 years earlier.

The loss of three legions was a catastrophe for Augustus. He had lost nearly 15,000 of his best soldiers at a time when Rome's forces were already overstretched. He is supposed to have regularly shouted out at times of depression, 'Quinctilius Varus, give me back my legions!' (Suetonius, *The Twelve Caesars*, Augustus, 23). Once again there was panic in Italy, and frantic efforts to organise troops. Arminius urged his allies to attack Roman Gaul, but King Marob refused to risk any offensive action. Tiberius quickly marched to the northern frontier and Drusus' son Germanicus led four legions as his second-in-command. Tiberius showed his usual efficiency in organising the defence of the Rhine and launched some punitive raids on the eastern bank. He decided, though, that it would be too great a risk to attempt to reoccupy the old province. He persisted with this cautious policy when he became emperor.

For the last five years of Augustus' reign, Tiberius was highly influential and his natural caution dominated Rome's military policy. Tiberius himself was now in his fifties and as an old soldier he rejected any further risks. Tacitus' account of this period suggests that the younger Germanicus was more adventurous, but that his uncle restrained his youthful ambition (Tacitus, *Annals*, II.25). Augustus did not achieve his dream of frontiers on the Elbe and the Danube: his plan made strategic sense, and perhaps the Roman Empire would have been even more wealthy and long-lasting if he could have achieved his goals. However, Tiberius had always been a general who was careful of his soldiers' lives, and his opinion was decisive.

Despite the failures of his last years, Augustus had won a great deal of land for the empire. The northern frontier was secure on the Danube and the Rhine, if not on the Elbe as he had hoped. In the east he had established a secure border on the Euphrates and had gained strategic control over the kingdom of Armenia. Thus he made sure that Rome possessed the initiative in her rivalry with Parthia. His imperial outlook was much closer to that of Julius Caesar than to the more cautious Tiberius. When Virgil in his *Aeneid* proclaimed that the gods had granted the Romans 'empire without borders' (*Aeneid*, I.279), he was simply reflecting the ideology of his day. Augustus' imperial vision cost the lives of many Roman soldiers and of even larger numbers of his foreign opponents. However, he succeeded in establishing the Roman Empire on secure borders that would not be challenged for hundreds of years.

CHAPTER 7

THE MYTH OF CAESAR AUGUSTUS

Augustus was not the first Roman politician to concern himself with the task of influencing opinion. The power that he acquired and the length of his reign meant that he developed the art of propaganda well beyond anything that his predecessors had attempted. Augustus understood how to win over the support of different classes of opinion. Once his popularity was assured, he made a great effort to influence the historical record of his actions. His concern for his political legacy was not simply personal vanity. Augustus' ambition was to set up a new system of government that would endure beyond his own lifetime. This required not merely careful legislation, but also the control of opinion. Augustus succeeded so well in this ambition that his system survived such erratic rulers as Caligula and Nero. Even when the Julio-Claudian dynasty came to an end, the new ruler Vespasian sought to model his rule on Augustus' system.

Augustus' proudly boasted that he had found Rome made of brick and left it made of marble (Suetonius, *The Twelve Caesars*, Augustus, 28; Cassius Dio, *Roman History*, 56.30.3). His extensive building programme was not simply designed to improve the look of the city: it was a clear statement of the power and wealth of the *princeps*. Augustus understood that the way to influence the mass of ordinary citizens was by the power of images. Only a minority of Romans would have read the detailed inscription of the *Res Gestae* or even worked their way through Virgil's

Aeneid, but they would all have been impressed by the number of Augustus' statues, by the Ara Pacis (the Altar of Peace), and by the temple of Mars Ultor (Mars the Avenger). The buildings that Augustus ordered were a direct explanation of his political ideology.

Augustus had first showed his flair for gaining the support of Roman citizens, when he celebrated funeral games for his adopted father in July 44 BC. When a comet appeared he declared this celestial phenomenon to be Caesar's personal star and that it was proof of the divine will that Julius Caesar should be declared a god. He ordered that this star should be added to Caesar's statues and put himself at the head of the popular cult of Divus Julius. From the beginning he made sure that his political message was easy to understand. He declared his *pietas*, his duty to protect the popular memory of his adopted father and proclaimed that he would seek vengeance for his father's murder. These persuasive slogans, combined with generous grants of money, helped him to win over the loyalty of the urban mob and, even more important, helped him to recruit large numbers of veteran soldiers. Augustus' popularity as Caesar's son made it very difficult for rivals such as Antony to order his troops to attack him.

One public building that had a clear political purpose was Augustus' mausoleum. Despite his youth, he ordered the construction of his family burial site in 32 BC in the city of Rome, north of the old city wall. The work on this building was conveniently timed to emphasise the contrast between his loyalty to Rome's traditions and Antony's betrayal of Roman values. Antony's last will and testament had apparently revealed his wish to be buried in Alexandria with Cleopatra. Augustus was making a clear statement that he considered Rome to be the centre of the empire. Once the mausoleum was finished it

3 Augustus' mausoleum

became a symbol of the power of Augustus' family. The central core of it still survives, but the original building was much more impressive. It was 77 metres in diameter and 45 metres tall. Augustus created large parks around the mausoleum to encourage the inhabitants of Rome to witness the glories of his family. The funerals of Augustus' family became personal tragedies for the Roman people and each elaborate ceremony stressed the bond that the new dynasty had with their city. Successively Marcellus, Agrippa, Drusus, Lucius and Gaius were buried in Augustus' tomb.

In 13 BC the Senate ordered the construction of the famous Ara Pacis, near Augustus' mausoleum on the Campus Martius (Field of Mars). This monument was eventually completed by 9 BC and still survives as one of the artistic wonders of the Roman world. It gives us a useful insight into the image Augustus wished to project. The monument celebrated Augustus' achievement in bringing peace to Rome and the new prosperity that the Italians were finally enjoying as a result of the first prolonged period of political stability in a hundred years. A famous panel pictures the goddess Mother Earth bestowing a bounty of prosperity upon the inhabitants of Italy; another panel recalls Virgil's *Aeneid*, which had been published merely six years before, and depicts Aeneas sacrificing a sow to the *penates* (household gods) after his arrival in Latium. The famous processional frieze shows Augustus acting as a priest, followed by his family and the Senate. The whole work remains a powerful record of the picture Augustus presented to his subjects.

Augustus ordered a large number of statues of himself, his family and his followers to be erected in Rome and the other cities of Italy. Artists flocked from Greece to benefit from the

4 *The Ara Pacis*

5 *Detail of the Prima Porta statue*

generosity of the new patron. He took particular care to project himself as an energetic and powerful ruler, as we can see from surviving statues such as the statue of Augustus from Livia's villa at Prima Porta just outside the city of Rome. This statue was a marble copy of a bronze original designed to celebrate Augustus' achievement in recovering the lost standards of Crassus and Antony from the Parthians. The statue is over 2 metres tall to create an imposing picture of the emperor. Augustus' youthful appearance is modelled on images of Alexander the Great to emphasise his success in war. Cupid rides on a dolphin next to his right foot to remind the viewer of Augustus' claim to descend from the goddess Venus through the Julian family. On the breastplate the sculptor depicted the return of the legionary standards by the Parthians in 20 BC using intricate but identifiable images.

Augustus' most ambitious political building programme in Rome was the Augustan Forum, completed in 2 BC. This forum was centred on a new temple to Mars Ultor, which celebrated Augustus' vengeance on the murderers of Julius Caesar and his victory over Cleopatra at Actium. Augustus had vowed to complete this temple 40 years earlier, after the battle of Philippi. Two colonnades flanked the imposing temple and the forum was the setting for a large number of statues. The focal point was a statue of Augustus himself, and in the interior of the temple there were statues to Mars, Venus and Divus Julius. In the centre of the courtyard in front of the temple was another statue of Augustus, riding in a chariot drawn by four horses and carrying an inscription with his favourite title, 'Pater Patriae' (Father of his Country). Augustus finally accepted this title in 2 BC, at the same time as the dedication of this forum; the title was also inscribed on Augustus' house on the Palatine Hill and in the chamber of the Senate House.

Augustus' imperial residence on the Palatine Hill was also built with political objectives in mind. An important part of Augustus' image was his moderation as a ruler. Antony and Cleopatra might celebrate their wealth and power with extravagant consumption; Augustus preferred to represent himself as an example of traditional Roman modesty and self-control. His diet was restrained and he spent much of his time on civil administration and religious worship. His wife Livia was a central part of this traditional family image. Although she was an important adviser for Augustus and notorious for her political scheming, she presented the impression of a modest Roman *matrona*, engaged in respectable pursuits such as managing the household and spinning cloth. In line with this portrayal, Augustus' residence may have been in Rome's most desirable quarter, the Palatine, but the size and decoration of the house were relatively modest by the standards of luxury of the nobility in the late republic. It was Augustus' successors, including Caligula and Nero, who created the later image of imperial opulence.

Augustus' building programme was massively extensive. He spends much of the *Res Gestae* describing the temples he had built throughout the empire. In one year alone (his sixth consulship in 28 BC), he claimed to have restored 82 temples (*Res Gestae*, 28). The civil wars and the triumvirate had caused the neglect and even the destruction of temples and civic buildings. Augustus' development programme was a symbol of stability and his intentions for the future. The Augustan government did not neglect works of engineering. Agrippa was given specific responsibility for the maintenance of Rome's water supply; although he had served a number of times as consul, he took on the position of aedile and ordered the building of two new aqueducts: the Aqua Virgo and the Aqua Iulia. These improved the public water supply and allowed the building of vast new bathhouses named in Agrippa's honour on the Campus Martius.

One project with an ironic function was Augustus' construction of the Saepta Iulia. Julius Caesar had originally begun this building to serve as a site for the large popular assemblies. Now under Augustus' regime voting was much less important and so this new complex was used for public markets and as a place for comfortable walks in shelter. The political message for the inhabitants of Rome behind this vast building programme was obvious. Augustus represented himself as the guardian of stability and prosperity. His power and that of the state were identical.

The building programme was only one part of Augustus' agenda to project his political message to the masses. He had a shrewd understanding of the power of ceremony. In 17 BC he organised the celebration of the *ludi saeculares* (secular games), which were Rome's most important public festival. The Latin word *saecularis* meant 'change of age', in terms of the maximum span of a human life, rather than 'non-religious' (as in our modern English word secular). The basic principle behind these games was that they should be celebrated every hundred years, or when there was no one left alive who could remember the previous games. The message of a new age fitted in very conveniently with Augustus' ideology. The Etruscan priests indicated that the conditions had been fulfilled, and Augustus ordered that all the free inhabitants of Rome, both men and women, should take part in the games. After Virgil's death in 19 BC, Horace had become Rome's most celebrated living poet and he wrote his famous poem the *Carmen Saeculare* to celebrate the occasion. Horace called upon Apollo, Augustus' patron god and Diana, Apollo's sister, and asked them to protect the people of Rome and their benevolent ruler Augustus.

Augustus was not simply concerned to preserve the support of the urban plebs in Rome. They were his natural constituency anyway and, while their support was useful, he had to consider other groups as well. Julius Caesar had possessed the same ability to win popularity from the poorer citizens, but this had not prevented him from being assassinated by upper-class senators. Augustus understood the importance of securing and maintaining his popularity with the upper classes. He was also very interested in his historical legacy. Thus Augustus made unprecedented efforts to promote a positive image of his rule through the literature of the period. The Augustan age is remembered as much for its literature as its other achievements.

As we have seen, Augustus' close supporter Maecenas made a deliberate effort to cultivate personal friendship with the best poets of the age such as Propertius, Virgil and Horace to persuade them tacitly to support Augustus. Augustus himself also took a personal interest in Maecenas' literary circle and attended public recitations on a regular basis. He even invited his particular favourites, Virgil and Horace, to give private recitations before the imperial family. Thus the poets strove to gain the favour of the wealthiest and the most assiduous patron in Rome. Virgil had originally written in praise of Gaius Asinius Pollio and Horace had supported the senator Fabius Maximus, but they both moved to support Augustus and his new government. There is no reason for us to believe that this support was insincere. Neither Virgil nor Horace belonged to great republican families. They must have been grateful for the new security and prosperity in Italy. The rewards for writing poetry supportive of the government were generous; both Virgil and Horace became wealthy landowners in middle age. Maecenas and Augustus were shrewd enough not to demand simple panegyric or propaganda. Rather, it appears that Maecenas' ambition was to sponsor a new age of Roman literature, aiming to rival the greatness of Periclean Athens or the age of Homer and Hesiod. Virgil and Horace became enthusiastic supporters of this plan.

Even before joining Maecenas' circle, Publius Vergilius Maro —better known today as Virgil—had reflected the political background in his earliest surviving poems, the *Eclogues*, which were written in around 40 BC (scholars are not able to date these poems exactly). Eclogues I and IX refer to the confiscation of farms in Italy, while Eclogue IV was probably inspired by the temporary reconciliation between Octavian and Antony at their meeting at Brundisium in 40 BC arranged by Maecenas. Around 38 BC Virgil joined Maecenas' group of poets and became closer to Octavian's inner circle. From 38 BC to 29 BC Virgil worked on the *Georgics*, a work of didactic poetry in four books, celebrating the virtues of traditional Italian farmers.

Virgil's *Aeneid* (written between 28 BC and 19 BC) is the most famous production of Augustan literature. It was a long Latin epic poem designed to rival the works of Homer. Virgil wrote this poem to be the great work of Latin literature celebrating the Augustan age, as Maecenas and Augustus had hoped. However, Virgil made Aeneas the Trojan the main hero of the work. The Homeric setting of the poem ensured its distance from the Roman context and so the poem avoided seeming too ingratiating or false. Yet Virgil's hero is clearly a prototype for the ideal Roman and is meant to embody the qualities of courage, clemency, justice and piety that Augustus had claimed as his cardinal virtues and which the Senate had inscribed on the shield in the Senate House in Augustus' honour. Furthermore, by means of passages presented as prophecy, Virgil refers directly to Augustus on a number of occasions.

The most informative of these passages comes in Book VIII of the *Aeneid*, when the god Vulcan hands over to Aeneas divine armour to help him for his forthcoming battle against the enemy champion, Turnus (*Aeneid* VIII 626f.). Vulcan has decorated the shield with incidents from the history of Rome, which he knows about because of his divine foreknowledge. In the centre of the shield Vulcan has portrayed Augustus' victory over Antony and Cleopatra at Actium. This battle is represented as the climax of Roman history and the summit of the Roman achievement. Virgil describes the gods of Rome gaining the upper hand over the gods of Egypt. He gives the most detailed description of Augustus' patron god, Apollo of Actium, drawing his bow against the Egyptian enemy. Cleopatra is pale with the pallor of approaching death and does not see the snakes at her back. Antony is guilty of the wicked outrage of subordinating himself to a foreign wife. Virgil then moves to a description of Augustus' triumphal procession in Rome, which was held in 29 BC, only ten years before the publication of the *Aeneid*. The streets are thronged with joyous crowds as Augustus consecrates 300 shrines throughout the city. Augustus then inspects the defeated nations of the east from his seat next to the altar of Apollo.

In the *Aeneid* Virgil makes another interesting reference to an even more recent event. In Book VI Aeneas journeys to the Underworld to see his dead father Anchises, who will tell him important prophecies for his future. When Aeneas meets Anchises, his father shows him a parade of future Romans who are waiting to be born in the upper world. Anchises uses hyperbole to explain that Augustus will extend Rome's empire beyond the Indus, which had marked the limits of the conquests of Alexander, and that he will bring back the golden years to Latium, which is very much the same message as that conveyed by the Ara Pacis (*Aeneid*, VI.792–800). However, the most poignant moment of the parade of heroes comes when Anchises describes a young man with a noble appearance, but downcast expression. We are told that this young man would make the Roman race too powerful if he was allowed to grow to maturity, and that the gods would grow envious. He describes the noise of mourning as the Romans carry the body of this young man to his mausoleum on the Field of Mars by the banks of the Tiber. Anchises ends his description by saying that if the young man is allowed to live at all, '*tu eris Marcellus*' (you will be Marcellus) (*Aeneid*, VI.883), and thus we at last find out that he is describing Augustus' nephew Marcellus who died in 23 BC only four years before Virgil's own death and the publication of the *Aeneid*.

The effect is moving, even for a modern reader, and must have been very powerful for those who had witnessed Marcellus' funeral. An anecdote from Servius Maurus Honoratus, a fourth-century AD commentator on Virgil, describes him as reading out

6 *The Theatre of Marcellus*

this passage to Augustus and his family at a private recitation. Marcellus' mother Octavia is supposed to have fainted at the mention of his name. Funeral masks of distinguished ancestors were an important feature of Roman funerals, and the description of Marcellus' great ancestors before the elegiac description of his own death gives the whole passage the atmosphere of a Roman funeral. Anchises ends by asking Aeneas to give him lilies and to leave him to scatter red roses. Thus the passage ends with the funeral rites for the young prince (*Aeneid*, VI.883–6).

We can see how important the *Aeneid* was to Augustus by the story surrounding its publication. Virgil died in 19 BC. He had reached the end of his poem, but he intended to spend some time editing it. The story goes that Virgil asked that his manuscript should be burned. However, Augustus ordered his servants to bring the text to him. He read it and ordered that it should be published. This story is most likely to be an amusing legend, but what is certain is that Augustus made great efforts to see that as many Romans as possible read the *Aeneid*. It quickly achieved classic status and became Rome's most widely read work of literature. It was studied in schools and even became the essential text for foreigners wishing to learn Latin.

Augustus made such an effort to circulate the *Aeneid* because it put forward a patriotic message that he wished to spread. No poem would have had as dramatic an effect on popular opinion as his building programme and his great spectacles, but it would have had some positive impact among the educated classes. Above all Augustus wanted Virgil to write for posterity. Maecenas and Augustus realised that the works of poetry would last beyond the lifetime of the author and the patron. Virgil was well rewarded for his work and by the time of his death he owned property worth around 10 million sesterces (very roughly equivalent to £10 million). Considering that students still study the *Aeneid* in schools and colleges, Augustus received great value for his money.

After Virgil's death the most important poet in Maecenas' circle was Virgil's contemporary, Quintus Horatius Flaccus, known to the modern world as Horace. Horace had led a colourful life. He was the son of a wealthy freedman from the provincial town of Venusia who had recognised young Horace's creative talent and had managed to afford an excellent education for his son in one of the best schools in Rome. Horace had then moved to Athens to continue his studies, but after the assassination of Julius Caesar he had joined the forces of Marcus Brutus, inspired by the thought of defending the republic. He had risen to the rank of *tribunus militum* (tribune of soldiers) before Marcus Brutus' eventual defeat. Horace later humorously describes how he had managed to survive the battle of Philippi by throwing away his shield. He benefited from Octavian's *clementia* towards middle-ranking officers and became an enthusiastic supporter of the Augustan regime.

Even before Virgil's death, Horace had been Rome's leading lyric poet and wrote four books of *Odes* that contained plenty of positive references to Augustus and praise for traditional Roman values (e.g Horace, *Odes*, I.37.6–12, III.1.48, III.6.1–5, III.24.19–22). In 18 BC he was chosen to write the *Carmen Saeculare*, a poem specially prepared for the *ludi saeculares*. For the next ten years Horace was a close friend to Maecenas and frequently entertained him on his Sabine farm. Augustus and Maecenas made sure that Horace was well rewarded for his support and he became a wealthy landowner. Horace survived Maecenas by only a few months and on his death in 8 BC, Horace bequeathed his lands to Augustus in recognition of his generous sponsorship.

Augustus was not able to achieve such a smooth relationship with another of Rome's most gifted poets. Maecenas certainly continued to demonstrate his eye for talent when he sponsored Publius Ovidius Naso, better known as Ovid. Ovid was born from a more prominent family than Horace or Virgil. His family had been active supporters of Augustus in the town of Sulmo, and hoped that Ovid would rise to senatorial rank. Ovid preferred to devote himself to poetry, which he wrote rapidly and with immaculate style. Ovid did produce a number of poems that referred positively to Augustus and his new government and which celebrated traditional Roman values (e.g. *Metamorphoses*, XV.852–70; *Fasti*, I.223–4). However, his more famous collections of poems, *Amores* (The Loves) and *Ars Amatoria* (The Art of Love) included witty advice on how to seduce young ladies of quality. Augustus frowned on this material as counter to the spirit of his social legislation, which we will look at in the next chapter. After his fall from favour, Ovid protested that his work was simply parody and that his own life was modest. Augustus was not amused, particularly as Ovid may well have been involved in the disgrace of Augustus' granddaughter, the younger Julia in AD 8.

Even though he frequently praised Augustus and his regime, Ovid was ordered to the palace and commanded by Augustus personally to go into exile. There was no need for a trial in the last years of Augustus' principate. Authority could be fearful, as well as benevolent. Ovid departed to Tomi in the province of Moesia (modern Bulgaria) on the shores of the Black Sea. Despite his pleas in his late works, *Tristia* (Sadness) and *Epistulae ex Ponto* (Letters from the Black Sea), he was never allowed home even after Augustus' death, and this most urbane of poets did not see Rome again. Ovid never reveals the exact reason for his exile, but mysteriously says in the *Tristia* that it was caused by '*carmen et error*' (a poem and a mistake) (*Tristia* 2. 207). The poem he refers to is most likely the *Ars Amatoria* and the mistake may well have been failure to tell the *princeps* about the antics of his granddaughter and her fashionable set. One might argue that Augustus was the poorer for dismissing Ovid: even after his exile, Ovid was the most popular poet in Rome. His *Metamorphoses*, an epic in 15 books, was a great success and is still widely read today. It is the most accessible of all Latin poems for a student beginning to read poetry in the original language. Ovid is also our most important source for Greek myths and legends. In the final book of the *Metamorphoses* he states that he has completed a work that neither Jupiter's anger nor fire nor iron, nor hungry time can obliterate (*Metamorphoses*, XV.871–9). Ovid's exile reveals the limits of Augustus' claim to have restored liberty and to have created a generous and merciful state. The wit of the poet has survived the anger of the autocrat.

CHAPTER 8

SOCIAL ENGINEERING
'BACK TO BASICS'

Once Augustus had safely established his power, he was determined to make his mark on Roman society. He shared the prevailing sentiment that the Roman senators of his era had fallen short of the standard of behaviour set by previous generations. The historian Sallust had argued that the extravagance of the upper class had been an important cause of the civil wars. As a *popularis* and a supporter of Julius Caesar, he blamed Sulla for the moral decline. He believed that increasing rewards for the wealthy had led them to be corrupted by the example of the Greek east and that Sulla had seduced his centurions and soldiers with lax discipline and excessive rewards (*War with Catiline*, X.4–7).

It was not merely the *populares* who objected to the decadence of Roman society. Cicero's writings harked back to the golden age of the generation that had beaten Hannibal, and despaired of the excessive luxury of some of his colleagues in the Senate. Poets such as Horace and Virgil begged Augustus to act as a physician and heal the fevered state. No doubt they were reflecting the official line, but there is every reason to believe they were sincere. Thus Augustus was able to rely on a socially conservative consensus in his attempt to reform Roman society.

Augustus' upbringing in the provincial town of Velitrae contributed to his conservative attitudes. He did not share the social sophistication of Julius Caesar, who was notorious as one of Rome's most prolific adulterers. Amid the prosperity of empire he wished to restore the traditional values of rural Italy. Virgil's *Aeneid* reflects these same conservative values. In the Underworld Aeneas finds a place in the punishment zone of Tartarus for adulterers, those who cheat their way to excessive wealth and those who betray their masters. In Elysium the gods reward brave soldiers who died for their country, faithful priests and honest artists and poets. In an informative simile in Book VIII, Virgil's greatest praise for a wife is that she looks after her slaves diligently, keeps her husband's bed chaste, brings her sons to manhood and supports the life of the household by the humble work of spinning thread on the wheel (*Aeneid*, VIII.408–13).

Although social legislation was popular with Augustus' conservative base, this did not mean that the upper class were prepared to change their behaviour. Augustus' supporters formed a new ruling elite. Many of them had reached the pinnacle of wealth and power after a desperate struggle, and they wanted to enjoy their position. The younger generation became even more difficult. They had not witnessed the carnage of the civil wars and took their prosperity and security for granted. In the second half of Augustus' reign, this tension was particularly obvious.

One of Augustus' concerns was the regulation of the process of the freeing of slaves, known as manumission. The growth of the Roman Empire had led to a huge influx of slaves to Italy. This development made a dramatic impact on the economic and social life of Augustan Italy. The wealthiest Romans owned large numbers of slaves in their luxury villas and would use an even greater number to farm their estates. Ever since the second century BC this flood of new slaves had made it difficult for the smaller landowners to compete, and there had been a steady migration of the free population from the countryside to the city of Rome and the other Italian towns. The Romans exploited their slave population effectively; Roman society was cruel even by ancient standards, and the most unfortunate slaves suffered a dreadful fate. Conditions on many of the *latifundia* (large farms) were often terrible, but perhaps the very worst life for slaves was working in the mines. Strabo describes the mercury mines as particularly lethal, and the average life expectancy for a slave there was six months (Strabo, *Geography*, 12.3.40).

The Romans did allow some slaves to have the chance to improve their lives. We should not see this as evidence of Roman humanitarianism, but rather as a shrewd calculation of self-interest. There were some skilled slave professions, such as household stewards or farm managers, where incentives rather than cruelty provided more effective motivation. Thus the Romans created a system whereby freed slaves could achieve a restricted form of citizenship. If they had freeborn offspring, these children could become full citizens, although they would usually live at the bottom of the social ladder. One heart-warming example of social mobility was the poet Horace. His father had been a slave, but he had earned his freedom before Horace's birth. Horace described how his father saved up enough money from his work as an auctioneer to give his intellectual son the best possible education (Horace, *Satires*, I.6.76–90). His father even travelled with him to Rome to act as his *paidagogus* (personal tutor), a role that a Greek slave would usually perform. As described in the previous chapter, as a result of his literary success and his friendship with Maecenas and Augustus, Horace became one of the most famous Augustan poets.

One advantage of this system of manumission was that it gave Rome a continual supply of new citizens. Unlike the Greek city-states of Athens or Sparta, Rome was always able to draw upon plentiful manpower for its armed forces. Many of the sons of freed slaves must have ended up in the armies of Antony and Octavian. We know that both Sextus Pompeius and Agrippa used freedmen or even conscripted slaves to row their galleys. However, by 20 BC there was widespread disquiet that the process of manumission had become too easy. Augustus was concerned that too many non-Italians had become citizens as freed slaves.

Thus Augustus secured three different laws over a period of 20 years dealing with this issue. The first law, the *Lex Junia*, cannot be dated exactly, but a plausible argument places it in 17 BC (based on Gaius, *Institutes*, I.22). The *Lex Junia* covered informal manumission. Because the formal freeing of slaves was an expensive and complicated procedure, it had become far more common for masters simply to free their slaves informally. Augustus' new law gave these freed slaves a legally defined status. They were to be regarded as free, but were denied full rights as citizens. The *Lex Junia* granted them 'Latin rights', which gave them the same status as the Romans had previously granted to their allied communities in Italy before they gave them full citizenship after the Social War. They were also restricted in their ability to dispose of their property. If they had freeborn offspring, those children would have the status of freeborn Roman citizens.

Augustus passed his next law concerning the manumission of slaves in 2 BC. The *Lex Fufia Caninia* dealt with the process by which masters might free slaves in their last will and testament. This form of manumission was attractive for slaves as it gave them full freedom as Roman citizens. It was also popular with masters because they did not feel the cost of manumission in their own lifetime and they could ensure that they had a well-attended and dramatic funeral as the freed slaves could be relied upon to play their part at this ceremony. Thus the *Lex Fufia Caninia* created a sliding scale by which the number of slaves a master could free in his will was restricted to a proportion of the number he already owned. For example a master owning 250 slaves was allowed to free a maximum of 50 in his will, and no master was allowed to free more than 100 slaves. This law had some effect in limiting the most common form of manumission and slowing the growth in the number of freed slaves.

In AD 4 Augustus organised the *Lex Aelia Sentia*, which went further to limit the number of freed slaves. This law covered the process by which masters could grant freedom to their slaves in their lifetime. It prevented any slave who had been severely punished either by his master or the state from gaining Roman citizenship. If he was ever freed, he was compelled to live more than 100 miles from the city of Rome. The law also provided age limits both for masters to free slaves and for the slaves who could be freed. Any master who wished to free his slaves had to be over 20 years of age. The slaves themselves had to be over the age of 30. Exceptions were only allowed to this rule in unusual circumstances. These three laws had a significant effect in stemming the numbers of slaves becoming citizens, and there is no evidence that later emperors felt a need to address this issue further.

Augustus found it much more difficult to reform the behaviour of the upper classes. He was eager to improve the status of marriage and to raise the birth rate among the senatorial elite and the equestrian upper-middle class. His most controversial proposal was his law to make adultery a criminal offence. Wealthy Romans frequently kept slave mistresses or used the services of foreign courtesans. There was no social stigma attached to this, and this behaviour did not come under Augustus' legislation. The Romans did have a strict social taboo against seducing the wives or daughters of citizens. This was regarded as malicious harm against a fellow Roman. However, it was regarded as essentially a private matter until Augustus' legislation. In 18 BC Augustus passed the *Lex Julia de Adulteriis Coercendis* (Julian Law Concerning the Punishment of Adultery). This law required a husband to divorce his wife, if he could prove that she had committed adultery. He could then prosecute both her and her lover. If convicted, they would be exiled to different islands and would lose a large part of their property.

There was a potential element of hypocrisy in this legislation. We have already seen Antony's allegation that Augustus himself pursued a number of affairs with married women, although this is of course a biased source. Augustus had certainly shown scant regard for the conventions of Roman marriage when he had removed Livia from her husband and married her when she was pregnant with her previous husband's child. Like many modern politicians, Augustus was content to pursue a policy of do what I say, not what I do. However, the image of the mature Augustus was strongly moralistic. He presented his family as upholding traditional Italian values, and he praised his wife Livia before the Senate for her modesty.

There is little evidence that Augustus' law against adultery had any positive effect on Roman society. Future emperors would be just as concerned about lax behaviour as Augustus had been. Far from returning to the morals of their ancestors, the upper class continued to behave much as before. The very worst scandals encroached on Augustus' closest family. Augustus' daughter and only natural child Julia had first married Marcellus, Augustus' nephew. After his death in 23 BC, Julia married Agrippa in 21 BC. Agrippa and Julia had five children, including Gaius and Lucius, whom Augustus adopted and named as his heirs. Agrippa died in 12 BC, and his last son Agrippa Postumus was born after his death. Augustus had then ordered Tiberius to marry Julia, but this led to disaster. Unhappiness in this new marriage was one of the reasons that Tiberius gave up his position as the second most powerful man in the empire and retired to Rhodes in 6 BC. Julia did not accompany him, and in 2 BC Augustus' agents brought him evidence that his daughter Julia had engaged in adulterous affairs with several aristocrats who were hostile to his government.

This scandal was probably the major personal shock of Augustus' reign. Augustus provided evidence before the Senate of Julia's scandalous conduct. She was convicted and sent to the barren island of Pandateria, where she lived for the rest of her life, outliving Augustus by one year. Augustus never saw her again. Her convicted lovers included five men from senatorial families. The most prominent was Iullus Antonius, the son of the triumvir Mark Antony. Despite his notorious father, his stepmother Octavia, Augustus' sister, had brought him up and he had become consul in 10 BC. The affair with Julia was more than a private scandal and it may well have included a plot to take over the throne. Iullus Antonius' family and prestige were strong enough to make him a genuine threat to Augustus and his grandsons. He was sentenced to death and then committed suicide. Julia's other noble lovers, including Sempronius Gracchus from the family of the Gracchi, were also exiled to remote islands. Tiberius was required to divorce Julia, but he was not brought back into favour for at least six more years, until after the death of Augustus' grandson Gaius. This was not the end of the scandal in Augustus' family. His granddaughter, also called Julia, was later exiled to an island on the charge of adultery.

At the same time as his law against adultery Augustus also passed the *Lex Iulia de Maritandis Ordinibus* (Julian Law Concerning Marriages between Different Classes). This law was designed to increase the birth rate of freeborn Italian citizens. It allowed Roman citizens, apart from senators and their sons, to marry freedwomen (women who had been born as slaves). The provisions of the law seem to indicate that even members of the equestrian class had been avoiding the expense of legitimate marriage by living with freedwomen partners. Augustus was so keen to increase the birth rate that he allowed these *equites* to marry their freedwomen mistresses, but he did not go so far as to apply the same leniency to senators. The law also restricted the rights of unmarried men and women to inherit property from outside their own family. This law became unpopular and Augustus had to bow to senatorial opinion near the end of his rule in AD 9 and amend it with the *Lex Papia Poppaea*. Ancient historians commented on the irony that Augustus' lack of success in encouraging senators to marry is demonstrated by the fact that both the consuls who proposed the law in the Senate and from whom the law took its name were bachelors (Cassius Dio, *Roman History*, LVI.10.3). Augustus attempted one other measure to encourage senators to have children. Candidates for political office were allowed to stand as many years before the legal minimum age as they had children. Two members of Augustus' own family set a positive example in this respect. As we have seen, Agrippa and Julia had five children in nine years of marriage. Later in Augustus' and in the early years of Tiberius' reign, Germanicus, the son of Livia's son Drusus, had six children with his wife Agrippina, the daughter of Agrippa and Julia. Both families appeared cursed, as they nearly all met premature and violent deaths.

All the evidence suggests that Augustus' attempts to encourage the birth rate among senatorial families were not successful. Later commentators remark that a large number of senators did not marry or have legitimate children. This lack of legitimate heirs led to the social phenomenon of legacy hunters. These ambitious young men would attach themselves to the service of a childless senator or a wealthy man and would try to ingratiate themselves with him, so that they would be named in his will. These legacy hunters continued to be unpopular during the rule of Tiberius, and Pliny also criticises them a century later (Pliny, *Letters*, II.20).

There was a strong contrast between Augustus' great success as a constitutional reformer and his failure to influence the moral climate of Rome. His attempts to restrict adultery led only to embarrassment within his own family. His efforts to increase the birth rate of the upper class had little effect and led to political difficulty. The only significant benefit these laws had was to raise revenue from confiscated inheritances, which was helpful for Augustus' plan to create a military treasury to fund the financial grants to soldiers on their retirement. Augustus may have hoped to bring about an era of more restrained behaviour. Instead, the next century saw the excesses of Caligula and Nero. Perhaps the lesson is that even the most determined legislator can do little to influence the follies of human behaviour.

CHAPTER 9

THE IMPERIAL FAMILY

Augustus made the crucial decision that his new regime would be centred on his family. This required subtle diplomacy since the Romans had not tolerated a royal dynasty since the age of the kings. However, there had been a strong dynastic element within the late republic. The Senate was virtually a hereditary class, and we have seen how difficult it was for a new man such as Cicero to win the consulship. Much of the appeal of a Roman politician would be based upon the achievements of his ancestors. Thus Cicero described his younger contemporary Domitius Ahenobarbus as 'consul designate from the cradle' (*Letters to Atticus*, IV). Augustus' position as the son of the deified Caesar was absolutely crucial for his popularity and authority. Family lineage was not merely important for a Roman politician's standing within the senatorial elite. It is a significant fact that the four most important *populares* of the last century of the republic (Tiberius and Gaius Gracchus, Julius Caesar and Clodius) were able to boast impeccable ancestry. The urban poor liked the power of a famous name. Both Julius Caesar and Clodius possessed a certain aristocratic panache along with the common touch, and it was this combination of attributes that made them such effective vote winners.

Thus Augustus was determined to develop a governing elite within his own family; and yet he had to do this in a way that would not offend his own supporters or the aristocrats who he wanted to join his party. His first step in this direction was his marriage with Livia. Although the circumstances surrounding this marriage were scandalous, Livia's Claudian lineage added additional lustre to Augustus' prestige. Despite his position as the son of Caesar, his own direct lineage from the Octavii was not especially impressive, so this connection was important in developing further links with the republican aristocracy. Livia's two sons, Tiberius and Drusus, enjoyed illustrious Claudian ancestry on both sides. Even if Augustus had not adopted them, they could have expected glittering careers in Roman politics. Tiberius seems to have enjoyed a much easier relationship with the great noble families than Augustus owing to his lineage. Augustus, on the other hand, had a natural rapport with the Italian middle class.

Augustus' daughter Julia, born in 39 BC, had an important part to play in his efforts to build up the image of an imperial family. Dynastic marriage had been central to the politics of the Roman Republic. Even such a strong personality as Cato gained a great deal of influence because he was related to so many of the great republican families by marriage. Augustus dictated Julia's marriages out of his political interest. Some historians have sympathised with Julia on this count, but it was the binding custom among upper-class Roman families and Julia would have had no expectation of being able to choose her own husband. Thus Augustus' decision that Julia should marry his 17-year-old nephew Marcellus in 25 BC was very significant. By that time Augustus himself was 38 years old and he and Livia had been married for 13 years without having any children together. The fact that Augustus did not divorce Livia to have sons with another wife certainly suggests that his marriage was of great importance to him both personally and politically. Thus Marcellus' marriage to Julia was a sign that he was being prepared as Augustus' eventual successor. By 23 BC Marcellus was serving as aedile as part of his apprenticeship in government and he was granted the right to stand for the consulship ten years in advance of the age limit. Augustus also intended that his stepsons Tiberius and Drusus would be major figures in his state, but they were only granted the right to the consulship five years before they reached the minimum age. However, Marcellus' death at the end of 23 BC, shortly after Augustus' recovery from a serious illness, caused a change of plan.

Agrippa had evidently been annoyed by Marcellus' prominence and for the next ten years he was the second most powerful man in the empire. Agrippa's talent for strategy and military organisation had been crucial to Augustus' rise to power, and he continued to play a major role in Augustus' government. In 21 BC Agrippa married Julia. He strengthened his position by arranging for Tiberius to marry his daughter Vipsania, his daughter by his first marriage to Caecilia Attica, the daughter of Cicero's friend Atticus. This marriage was happy, according to the sources, and they had a son named Drusus. Agrippa had been a friend of Octavian before his rise to power in 44 BC, and his loyalty was absolute but his undistinguished ancestry meant that he was dependent on his friend. His marriage to Julia certainly strengthened his prestige and, had Augustus died any time between 23 BC and 12 BC, it is likely that Agrippa would have succeeded him as the effective ruler of the empire. Agrippa's political position became even stronger in 18 BC when Augustus granted him the *tribunicia potestas*. This title marked him out as Augustus' chosen successor in the event of his premature death.

Agrippa and Julia had five children in their nine years of married life, despite Agrippa's absences on military campaigns. Augustus adopted their two eldest sons, Gaius and Lucius, in 17 BC, and this strengthened his bond with Agrippa. Now these two boys became the designated successors to the empire and the dynastic link between Augustus and Agrippa appeared secure. Meanwhile Tiberius and Drusus began their military careers. Tiberius enjoyed great success in Armenia in 20 BC when Augustus regained the lost standards from the Parthians, and both enjoyed military success on the northern frontier in their campaigns after 15 BC. They were honoured as royal princes and held the status as the third and fourth most important men in the empire, but they were not at the head of the line of succession at this stage.

This apparently stable structure began to topple with the death of Agrippa in 12 BC. Augustus now needed a deputy who could conduct complex military campaigns and take on the role as stepfather to his grandchildren. The obvious man was Tiberius. Augustus ordered him to divorce his wife Vipsania, who was of little political importance now her father had died, and required him to marry Julia. The marriage duly took place in 11 BC. Tiberius' brother Drusus had married Antonia, daughter of Mark Antony and Augustus' sister Octavia. Their two sons, Germanicus and Claudius, would play a very important part in the imperial succession in the next generation.

Augustus' response appeared to solve the problem, but the results were unfortunate. Tiberius was distraught that he was required to divorce Vipsania. Tiberius and Julia had been brought up in the same household as children, and would have known each other well. They were relatively close in age by the standards of Roman marriage as Tiberius was only three years older than Julia. Suetonius records that their marriage was initially happy but turned sour after their baby died in infancy (Suetonius, *The Twelve Caesars*, Tiberius, 7). While Tiberius was absent on difficult military campaigns in Pannonia and Germany, Julia became notorious for her affairs with upper-class Romans. Rumours suggested that some of these affairs dated back to Julia's marriage with Agrippa, so this might also explain Tiberius' reluctance to marry her, despite the honour that went with this alliance. Tiberius clearly found his position humiliating, especially as his marriage with Julia did not mark him out as Augustus' successor. His role was to safeguard the interests and position of Gaius and Lucius. As they grew to maturity it was clear that he would be moved aside, despite his great military achievements.

Augustus' family suffered another personal tragedy with the death of Tiberius' younger brother Drusus in 9 BC as he was returning from a successful campaign in Germany. Drusus was popular both with the Roman people and within the governing elite. He had also proved a successful and efficient military commander. The sources record that Tiberius was particularly saddened and that he personally accompanied his brother's coffin on its slow journey from the northern frontier back to Rome. This loss must have contributed to his state of mind over the next few years. By 6 BC Augustus was only 56 years old. It had been 37 years since his first consulship, but he was still a master politician and fully in control of the state. His health was better than ever and Tiberius must have despaired of his own position. Augustus had given him further honours by arranging for the Senate to grant him *tribunicia potestas*, but this did not change Tiberius' fundamentally subordinate position. Thus he made the dramatic decision to resign all his offices in 6 BC and to retreat into retirement to the island of Rhodes.

This decision must have come as a bombshell to Augustus. Tiberius was 37 years old and clearly the second man in the empire. One of Tiberius' pretexts for his retirement was that it made way for Gaius and Lucius. However, the boys were still only 14 and 11, and in no way ready to take on political office.

Augustus must have planned for Tiberius to continue to act as his main assistant for at least ten more years, and for Gaius and Lucius to be carefully presented to the Roman people as Tiberius and Drusus had been. Augustus made vigorous attempts to persuade Tiberius to change his mind, even resorting to threats. Only his mother, Livia persuaded him to allow Tiberius to carry out his plan.

Tiberius' resignation meant that Augustus had to change his policy of entrusting the most important military commands to central members of the imperial family. The main sources, such as Velleius, Suetonius and Cassius Dio, are so fascinated by the struggle for the succession that we are less well informed about political events and which commanders were conducting the main campaigns between 6 BC and AD 4. We do know that Augustus gave command of the army in Germany to Lucius Domitius Ahenobarbus, the consul of 16 BC, in these years. Augustus did have a marriage alliance with this prominent family as Domitius was married to one of the daughters of Mark Antony and Octavia. This alliance with the imperial family would prove profitable for the fame of the Domitii as the grandson of this Domitius was the Emperor Nero.

Augustus' tough action in response to the revelation of Julia's affairs in 2 BC described in the previous chapter was almost certainly the result of his determination to secure the succession for Gaius and Lucius. Augustus' plans could have been threatened if Iullus Antonius—who had the family and personal prestige to be an alternative emperor—had been able to marry Julia, but the disgrace of their mother had little effect on the progress of the young princes. In 5 BC Augustus accepted the consulship for the first time in many years to mark the occasion of Gaius taking on the toga of manhood. He did the same in 2 BC when Lucius came of age. Gaius was appointed *princeps iuventutis* (leader of the youth) which mirrored Augustus' title of *princeps senatus* (leader of the Senate). Gaius was also designated for the consulship five years in advance, which meant that he would take on the consulship in AD 1.

Augustus did not want the young princes to grow idle at home. Instead, he prepared a testing political apprenticeship for them. He needed to confirm his settlement with Parthia on the eastern frontier and to reassert Roman control over the border client kingdom of Armenia. Accordingly, he sent Gaius out to the east, just as he had sent Tiberius 20 years before. He also ordered Lucius to travel through Gaul to visit the armies in Spain and represent the imperial family there. However, Augustus' careful plans for the succession began to unravel. In AD 2 Lucius died of an illness in Massilia (Marseilles). His body was brought back and buried in Augustus' mausoleum.

Gaius assumed the consulship for AD 1 in Syria. There was clearly a great deal of tension between Gaius' entourage, headed by Marcus Lollius, and the retired Tiberius. Tiberius dutifully left Rhodes to meet his stepson, but Lollius and the rest of Gaius' supporters showed him little respect. One follower of Gaius was supposed to have offered at a banquet to bring back the exile's head (Suetonius, *The Twelve Caesars*, Tiberius, 13). Ambitious Romans certainly saw Gaius as the man of the future and believed that Tiberius' best days were behind him. When Lollius died of an illness, Publius Sulpicius Quirinius, who was less hostile to Tiberius, replaced him as Gaius' chief of staff. Quirinius is famously mentioned in Luke's gospel as the governor of Syria. Tiberius now asked Augustus if he could return from Rhodes to Rome. Livia also petitioned her husband to grant this request. Augustus sought Gaius' approval for this measure, which must have been humiliating for Tiberius. Tiberius did return to Rome, but played no part in public life.

As we have seen, Gaius' negotiations in the east initially went well, but he was seriously wounded putting down an Armenian uprising and never recovered from his injuries. He attempted to return to Rome, but died in Lycia in southern Turkey in AD 4.

Augustus had lost both his heirs in the space of two short years. Agrippa Postumus was the last surviving son of Agrippa and Julia, but he was not regarded as a candidate for the imperial succession. He was considered bad tempered and aggressive (Tacitus, *Annals*, I.4). Cassius Dio records that he called himself Neptune and spent much of his time fishing (*Roman History*, LV.32). Thus Tiberius became the obvious candidate to be Augustus' heir. Robert Graves constructed an elaborate conspiracy theory in his novel *I Claudius*, suggesting that Livia was behind the deaths of Gaius and Lucius in order to secure the succession for her son Tiberius. A number of ancient historians, including Tacitus and Cassius Dio, do discuss this possibility (Tacitus, *Annals*, I.3; Cassius Dio, *Roman History*, LV.10) but such a theory is deeply implausible since it assumes that Augustus would have been too naive to uncover such a plan. The risks for Livia and Tiberius would have far outweighed any chance of success.

Augustus now made his peace with Tiberius. Even now, though, he imposed limits on Tiberius' succession. He adopted Tiberius as his son, and again granted him the *tribunicia potestas*, which was a clear indication of the intended succession. However, he required him to adopt his nephew, Drusus' son Germanicus, as his heir, despite the fact that Tiberius had a son of his own, also called Drusus. The likely explanation for this is that Germanicus' mother Antonia was the daughter of Octavia and Mark Antony, and thus had a direct blood link to Augustus' family. Also he was married to Agrippina, the daughter of Agrippa and Julia, and thus his children were Augustus' own great-grandchildren.

Tiberius accepted these terms and the two adoption ceremonies took place in June AD 4.

In the last ten years of his reign Augustus had great need of Tiberius' military abilities. In AD 6 Tiberius and Germanicus led the Roman forces in putting down a major revolt in the new province of Pannonia. It took three years of hard fighting to suppress this rebellion. Suetonius described it as the hardest Roman campaign since the war against Hannibal (Suetonius, *The Twelve Caesars*, Tiberius, 16). Not long after this revolt was subdued, as we have seen, Varus suffered his disaster in the Teutoburgian forest. Tiberius moved in to secure the frontier on the Rhine. By AD 12 the situation was secure enough for Tiberius to lead his forces back to Rome to celebrate a triumph for his campaigns in Pannonia and on the Rhine frontier.

The relationship between Augustus and Tiberius was undoubtedly tense in the last few years. Tiberius certainly had great respect for Augustus' civil policy and followed his precedents closely when he became emperor. However, he must have been deeply disgruntled about the way he had been treated and well aware that he was by no means Augustus' first choice as successor. In fragments from surviving letters recorded by Suetonius from these years, Augustus constantly reassured Tiberius how indispensable he was (Suetonius, *The Twelve Caesars*, Tiberius, 21). One senses that this reassurance would not have been necessary if the personal relationship between the two men had been closer.

Augustus' last political act was the publication of the *Res Gestae*. Suetonius records that he had deposited this document with the Vestal Virgins, and had ordered that it should be published on his death (Suetonius, *The Twelve Caesars*, Augustus, 101). Tiberius commanded that the text should be published in Latin and Greek throughout the empire. The *Res Gestae* has come down to us through three texts from Galatia (central Turkey). Though none of the individual texts is complete, enough survives for scholars to reconstruct virtually the full text in both languages. It records Augustus' accomplishments as he wished them to be remembered and is thus a crucial historical source. Augustus records his 13 consulships and the 21 times he was proclaimed *imperator*. He also records the vast sums that he spent on settling veteran soldiers and his extensive building programme. He mentions Gaius and Lucius and his grief that fortune had taken them away from him in their youth. He also records Tiberius' successes in Armenia and in Pannonia.

Augustus must have been aware by AD 13 that his health was failing. A consular law of AD 13 gave Tiberius equal powers to Augustus and proposed that they should conduct a census together. Augustus and Tiberius completed this census by May AD 14. In the summer Tiberius set out to visit the legions in Illyricum. Augustus initially travelled across Italy with him, but halted at the town of Nola, where his father had died. After falling ill, he recalled Tiberius from Illyricum. According to Velleius and Suetonius, Livia and Tiberius were present at Augustus' death (Velleius Paterculus, *History of Rome*, 123; Suetonius, *The Twelve Caesars*, Augustus, 98–9). The more sceptical Cassius Dio wrote that Augustus died before Tiberius returned and Livia concealed Augustus' death until Tiberius was able to take over power (Cassius Dio, *Roman History* LVI.30), but his account may originate from later sources hostile to Tiberius. Augustus died in the same room as his father on 19 August AD 14. Suetonius recalls that his last words were to Livia: 'Goodbye Livia: never forget our marriage' (*The Twelve Caesars*, Augustus, 99).

Tiberius organised Augustus' funeral following the arrangements that Augustus had made. Many mourners accompanied the procession that brought the body back from Nola to Rome.

A huge crowd flocked there for the funeral and all public business stopped on that day. Tiberius and Drusus delivered the funeral orations since Germanicus remained on the Rhine with the northern legions. Augustus' body was cremated, and as the fire burned an eagle was released into the sky. The Senate proclaimed Augustus a god, following the precedent set at the death of Julius Caesar, and ordered that all the provinces of the empire should celebrate the cult of Divus Augustus (the deified Augustus). The transfer of power to Tiberius was relatively smooth. The fact that Tiberius held the *tribunicia potestas* and had officially been granted equal powers to Augustus helped. Agrippa Postumus, a possible rival for power from within the imperial family, was killed on Augustus' orders, so Tiberius claimed. Germanicus declared his loyalty to Tiberius before his legions on the Rhine. The Senate duly acknowledged Tiberius as *princeps*, and voted him all the powers of Augustus. The fact that his power could be successfully transferred to his adopted son and heir was the final demonstration that Augustus had created a monarchy.

THE VERDICT

Augustus is undoubtedly one of the major figures of world history. His substantial political achievement was to create a system of government for the Roman Empire that lasted for centuries. The Julio-Claudian dynasty survived until AD 68 and the fall of Nero. A bitter civil war followed in AD 69, with four emperors swiftly succeeding each other. Eventually Vespasian established his hold on power and made every effort to build a new Flavian dynasty based on Augustus' model. In AD 96 Vespasian's son Domitian was assassinated and replaced by the Emperor Nerva. In order to confirm his power, Nerva adopted the popular general Trajan, and thus initiated a pattern of imperial succession that proved effective for most of the second century AD. Each emperor would nominate a successor on the grounds of his ability to rule the empire, and then adopt him as his son. This system proved remarkably successful until Marcus Aurelius named his natural son Commodus as his heir. Sadly Commodus was a weak and unpopular emperor on the lines of Caligula, Nero and Domitian. After he was assassinated in AD 180, a new era of civil disputes and conflicts between the leaders of the different parts of the empire arose. Rome was never so strong again.

Yet the western empire persisted until AD 476. Ironically, the last Western Roman emperor, who was deposed by the Goths, assumed the title Romulus Augustulus in a desperate attempt to gain credibility.

Augustus deserves credit for extending the boundaries of the empire. The frontiers that he created remained for the next two hundred years and allowed the Romans to benefit from permanent security. Claudius added Britain to the empire after AD 43 and Trajan added Dacia (modern-day Romania) in AD 105, but there were not many other permanent conquests after Augustus' death. Most emperors followed Tiberius' example and concentrated on holding onto the territory they already possessed, although the lure of military glory proved tempting to some.

The significance of Augustus' changes to the Roman state was obvious by the time of his death. When Tiberius took power the Roman legions on the northern frontier soon mutinied, to demand shorter terms of service and more pay. Tiberius sent Germanicus and Drusus to put an end to this. When they offered to refer the mutineers' demands to the Senate, the soldiers were scornful, replying that Augustus had always sent Tiberius to receive their requests and pass them on to the Senate and that Tiberius himself was using the same delaying tactics. These soldiers were well aware that the emperor held all the real power rather than the Senate. If the realities of power were so obvious to soldiers on a distant frontier, then they would have been clear to everyone in Rome, especially the senators themselves.

There are two main charges that can be levelled at Augustus. The first is that his successes did not justify the ruthless means by which he acquired power. The second is that his political system prepared the way for tyrannical and ineffective rulers such as Caligula, Nero and Domitian. The first accusation certainly has some weight: Augustus reached the summit of power because he was the shrewdest and most effective competitor in a cruel and brutal society. However, it is important to remember that his forebears and rivals—such as Cicero, Julius Caesar, Brutus and Antony—all practised and advocated similar violent action. One can at least say of Augustus that he had a political vision that was beneficial for most Roman citizens and provincial inhabitants of the empire, and that he had the determination to put this vision into practice. The second accusation explains the hostility of Tacitus to early emperors such as Augustus and Tiberius. Tacitus had begun his career in the difficult years of Domitian and was clearly nostalgic for the freer atmosphere of the republic. Under Augustus' system weaker rulers such as Caligula and Nero may have endangered the Senate, but they caused little harm to the population of Rome and Italy as a whole. The late republic with its golden generation of talented orators and generals led to destructive civil war throughout the empire.

Much of Augustus' success relied upon his superior political organisation. Other Roman statesmen, such as Julius Caesar and Cicero, had devoted care to the art of political communication, but Augustus developed this skill well beyond the level of his predecessors. The length of his rule and the extent of his power and wealth meant that he could manage contemporary opinion carefully and control the verdict of history on his reign. Maecenas' contact with the Augustan poets resembles the work of a modern communications director, even if his main aim was to establish Augustus' legacy, rather than to affect the politics of the day.

Augustus remained an autocrat to the end of his days. In his private moments in exile on the shores of the Black Sea Ovid must have bitterly complained at the arbitrary power of the great autocrat. Tiberius must also have been resentful about the way Augustus had treated him, despite his great services to the state. The great Claudians of the Republic were masters of their own destiny. In contrast, even the second man of the empire was dependent on the will of the *princeps*. Augustus' rule ended the great age of republican freedom in Rome. He deserves the title as the master of political manipulation in the ancient world.

The Family of Augustus

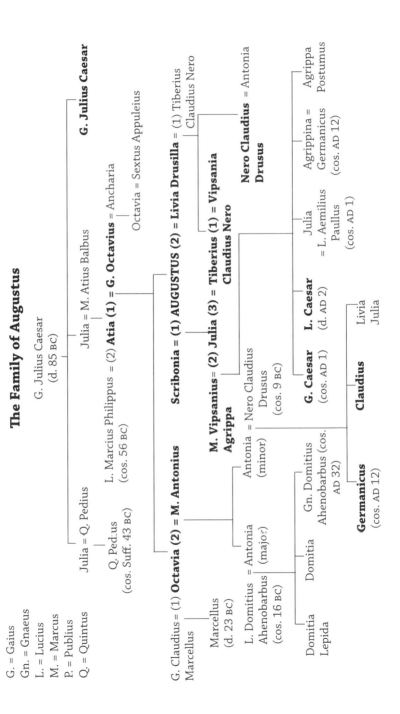

BIBLIOGRAPHY

Ancient sources

* indicates that an English translation is published by Penguin Books

Appian, *Roman History: The Civil War**

Augustus, *Res Gestae*

Caesar, *Gallic Wars**

Caesar, *Civil Wars**

Cassius Dio, *Roman History**

Cicero , *Catiline Orations**

Cicero, *Letters to Atticus**

Cicero, *Letters to his Friends**

Cicero, *Letters to Brutus**

Cicero, *Philippics**

Gaius, *Institutes*

Horace, *Carmen Saeculare**

Horace, *Epistolae**

Horace, *Odes**

Nicolaus of Damascus, *Life of Augustus*

Ovid, *Amores**

Ovid, *Ars Amatoria**

Ovid, *Fasti**

Ovid, *Metamorphoses**

Ovid, *Tristia**

Ovid, *Epistulae ex Ponto**

Pliny, *Letters**

Plutarch, *Life of Antony* (from *The Makers of Rome: Nine Lives*, London, Penguin Books).

Plutarch, *Life of Cicero* (from *Fall of the Roman Republic*, London, Penguin Books).

Polybius, *Histories**
Propertius, *Elegies*
Sallust, *The War with Catiline**
Sallust, *The War with Jugurtha**
Suetonius, *The Twelve Caesars**
Tacitus, *Annals**
Velleius Paterculus, *History of Rome*
Virgil, *Aeneid**
Virgil, *Eclogues**
Virgil, *Georgics**

Editions of all of the authors listed above, except for Nicolaus, are available in the original languages with facing English translations by the Loeb Classical Library, Harvard University Press, Cambridge, MA. English translations of most of the works can be found on the Lacus Curtius website (http://penelope.uchicago.edu/Thayer/E/Roman/home).

Modern sources

Bradley, P., *Ancient Rome; Using Evidence*, London, 1990.
Brunt, P.A. and J.M. Moore, *Res Gestae*, Oxford, 1967.
Eck, W., *Augustus*, Oxford, 1998.
Everitt, A., *Cicero*, London, 2001.
Everitt, A., *The First Emperor, Caesar Augustus and the Triumph of Rome*, London, 2006.
Holland, R., *Augustus, Godfather of Europe*, History Press, 2005.
Dessau, H. (ed.), *Inscriptiones Latinae Selectae*, 5 vols, Berlin, 1892–1916.
Jones, A.H.M., *Augustus*, London, 1970.
Levick, B., *Tiberius the Politician*, London, 1976.
Salmon, E.T., *A History of the Roman World, 30BC–AD138*, London, 1944.
Scullard, H.H., *From the Gracchi to Nero*, London, 1959.
Shotter, D., *Augustus Caesar*, London, 1991.
Southern, P., *Augustus*, London, 1998.
Syme, R., *Roman Revolution*, Oxford, 1939.
Syme, R., *History in Ovid*, Oxford, 1978.
Syme, R., *The Augustan Aristocracy*, Oxford, 1986.
Thorpe, M., *Roman Architecture*, Bristol, 1995.
Zancker, P., *The Power of Images in the Age of Augustus*, Michigan, 1988.

INDEX